Books by the Whiteheads

Method in Ministry

Shadows of the Heart:
A Spirituality of the Negative Emotions

The Promise of Partnership:
A Model for Collaborative Ministry

Community of Faith:
Crafting Christian Communities Today

Seasons of Strength:
New Visions of Adult Christian Maturing

A Sense of Sexuality

Christian Life Patterns

Method in Ministry
Theological Reflection
and Christian Ministry

—Revised and Updated—

James D. Whitehead
and
Evelyn Eaton Whitehead

SHEED & WARD
Franklin, Wisconsin

1999

Sheed & Ward
7373 South Lovers Lane Road
Franklin, Wisconsin 53132
1-800-266-5564

Grateful acknowledgment is made for permission to use the following materials which have appeared earlier in somewhat longer version: "Assisting Adults to Think Theologically," by Patricia O'Connell Killan, *Professional Approaches for Christian Educators (PACE),* February, 1993, volume 22, pp. 7–14, published by Brown ROA Publishing of Dubuque, Iowa; and "Mujerista Theology's Methods: Understandings and Procedure," Chapter 3 in *En La Lucha / In the Struggle: Elaborating a Mujerista Theology,* by Ada María Isasi-Díaz, copyright © 1993, Augsburg Fortress. Robert Schreiter's article "Reconciliation and the Church in China" originally appeared in TRI-POD, Vol. XII, no. 69 (May–June, 1992), pp. 44–52.

Printed in the United States of America

Library of Congress Cataloging-in-Publication Data

Whitehead, James D.
    Method in Ministry : theological reflection and Christian ministry / James D. Whitehead and Evelyn Eaton Whitehead.—Rev. and updated.
        p.   cm.
      ISBN: 1-55612-806-1
      1. Clergy—Office. 2. Clergy—Training of. I. Whitehead, Evelyn Eaton.
    BV660.2.W46.   1995
    253—dc20
                                                          95-8755
                                                          CIP

3 4 5 6 7 8 9 / 02 01 00 99

Contents

Part IV
Theological Reflection at Work

This book is dedicated to

John J. Egan
and
Jerome A. O'Leary

Mentors in Ministry

Preface to the 1995 Edition

METHOD IN MINISTRY APPEARED ORIGINALLY IN 1980. IN THE SUBSEQUENT fifteen years, our own understanding of theological reflection in ministry has been influenced and expanded by the work of Don Browning, Anne Carr, Virgilio Elizondo, Elisabeth Schüssler Fiorenza, Thomas Groome, Bernard Lee, James Poling, Rosemary Radford Ruether, Jack Shea, and David Tracy.

Many colleagues provided creative challenge and generous encouragement as we prepared the revision. Edward Foley at Catholic Theological Union in Chicago helped us see more clearly the special potency of the *listening* metaphor to describe the starting point of pastoral reflection. Robert Schreiter, also at C.T.U., and Michael Cowan at Loyola University in New Orleans deepened our awareness of the constitutive influence of culture.

Claire Lowery at Boston College reminded us of the links between theological reflection and the movement of discernment in spiritual direction. Jerry Handspicker at Andover-Newton Theological School highlighted the method's value in providing religious groups a safe structure for discussing potentially threatening differences in belief and behavior. Carl Dudley at Hartford Seminary challenged us to accentuate the vitality of the tradition as a resource in pastoral reflection and showed us practical ways to make our text more available to Protestant readers.

Marcel Dumestre (Director of the LIMEX graduate extension program of Loyola University New Orleans), Mary Ann Flanagan (Director of the Institute of Pastoral and Educational Ministry at Assumption University), Robert Kinast (Director of the Center for Theological Reflection in Florida), and Daniel Luby (Director of Adult Formation in the Diocese of Fort Worth) provided detailed comments on the method's strengths and limits in their own professional settings—and urged us to go forward with a revised edition.

We are equally indebted to Peter Buttitta, Patricia O'Connell Killen, Ada María Isasi-Díaz, and Robert Schreiter for allowing us to draw on their significant contributions to pastoral method for the chapters of Part Four. William Thompson and Eugene Ulrich have reviewed and up-dated their critical chapter on the use of Scripture in pastoral life. To Gene Ulrich we owe additional thanks for his generous involvement and ingenuity throughout the revision process.

The insight of all these gracious critics-and-friends has supported us during the writing effort and has substantively improved the revised text. We are most grateful!

J.D.W. & E.E.W.
January 1, 1995

• Introduction •

The Contemporary
Need for Method

THEOLOGICAL REFLECTION IN MINISTRY IS THE PROCESS OF BRINGING TO
bear in the practical decisions of ministry the resources of Christian
faith. In this book we propose both a model and a method for doing
theological reflection in ministry. In the model we indicate three
sources of information that are relevant to decision making in contemporary ministry: the Christian tradition, personal experience, and cultural resources. Faithful and effective pastoral activity depends on
the ability of Christians—and, in a special way, Christian ministers—to recognize and use the religiously significant insights avail
able in these three sources. In the method we suggest a three-step
process—attending, assertion, and pastoral response—through which
this information is clarified, coordinated, and allowed to shape pastoral action.

Theological reflection in ministry is not new. It is our conviction that effective ministry is always an ongoing dynamic of reflection and action. What we attempt to do here is to examine that process, to name its elements, and to suggest ways in which it can be
strengthened in the life of Christian ministry today.

While theological reflection in ministry is not new, its contemporary context is complex. Influenced by the explosion of information and the expansion of historical consciousness that mark this
century, ministers are more keenly aware of the limits of their own
knowledge. Recent research in Scripture has elaborated not only the
richness of this central source of Christian revelation, but its complexity and variation. The forms of worship, the understanding of
sexuality, the relation of the church to political life—in these and

other areas profound cultural changes have called into question earlier certitudes that were once the foundation of confident pastoral
action.

This exciting but often bewildering complexity in contemporary
Christian life heightens the need for a method of reflection: a systematic way to approach the various sources of religious information, one that leads not just to theoretical insight, but to pastoral
decision.   Christian ministry today requires a method of reflection
that is at once theological and practical.   As theological, it must attend confidently and competently to the resources of Scripture and
the historical tradition.   As practical, it must be more than theoretically sound; it must be able to assist a wide range of ministers in
their efforts to reflect and act in complex pastoral contexts.   The
method must be sufficiently clear and concrete that it can actually be
used by persons and groups in the church.   And it must be focused
on action; its process cannot end in religious insight but must be
open to pastoral response.   It is the need for such a method—at once
pastoral and theological—that is addressed in this book.

A Model and a Method

A *model* of theological reflection provides an image of the elements that are involved.   The model we discuss points to sources of
information that are important in pastoral decision making: Christian tradition, personal experience, and the resources of culture.   In
this understanding, theological reflection in ministry is the process
by which a community of faith engages the religious information
from these sources in pursuit of insight that will illumine and shape
pastoral response.

The *method* describes the dynamic or movement of the reflection. It outlines the stages through which the conversation proceeds.
The initial stage (attending) involves seeking out the diverse information residing, often in a partly-hidden fashion, in personal experience, the religious tradition, and the culture.   An intermediate stage
(assertion) instigates a dialogue among these sources of information
in order to clarify, challenge, and purify the insights and limits of
each.   The final stage (pastoral response) moves the reflection from
insight toward personal and communal action.

Situating the Method in Theological Context

The contribution of this method to the recent history of theological reflection can best be seen by recalling the reciprocal relationship of ministry and theology.   Theology intends an understanding

of faith that is ultimately practical. Its insights are meant to shape ministry. Ministry, on the other hand, is both shaped by theology and critiques the adequacy of theological formulations to the life of the church. Reflections on faith occur along this continuum, differing as they are more influenced by the immediacy of a pastoral concern or by the historical, scriptural, or philosophical complexity of a religious question. At the extremes of the ministry-theology continuum are styles of behavior familiar to every professional minister: theological reflection so abstract that its religious import is all but indiscernible and, at the other extreme, ministerial activity in which reflection enjoys almost no role.

Moving in from limit cases we encounter important models of theological reflection being developed. On the theology side of the continuum, the work of Paul Tillich, Bernard Lonergan, Elisabeth Schüssler Fiorenza and David Tracy and others has contributed significantly to our understanding of the nature of theological reflection.[1] Important as these contributions are, they remain too complex for all but the most astute minister. This is partly due to the scope of the inquiry, its length, and the conversation partners of such theological reflections. A theological reflection in systematic or fundamental theology on the faith statement, "Jesus is the Christ,"[2] will focus more on the historical interpretations of this phrase than on contemporary experiences of Jesus as the Lord. With such historical and exegetical scope this inquiry will require a relatively extended period of reflection. Finally, the conversation partners for such a reflection are history, philosophy, and hermeneutics—sources familiar to the professional theologian, but less so to others in the community of faith. Thus the scope, length of inquiry, and the conversation partners of this reflection suggest that this model will not likely be available to the minister. This is not to belittle such models of reflection, but only to suggest the need for their being complemented by other models of pastoral reflection.

On the ministry side of the continuum, two models of reflection suggest themselves. The first model, influenced by the methods of Clinical Pastoral Education (CPE), focuses on a specific pastoral concern through the report of a "critical incident." In a small group setting, a minister explores his or her own emotional and cognitive response and then, with the group, examines theological implications of the incident and considers possibilities for pastoral response. A second model of theological reflection, the case study method, begins with the preparation of a case, a pastoral question in its concrete historical setting. The case is presented to a group and its religious and pastoral implications are explored. The strength of

A Continuum of Theological Reflection

MINISTRY ← - - - - - - - - - - - - - - - → THEOLOGY

	immediate and concrete (this pastoral question)	*intermediate* (this pastoral question in its Christian and cultural context)	*broad* (a theological question in its philosophical and historical context)
scope	*immediate and concrete* (this pastoral question)	*intermediate* (this pastoral question in its Christian and cultural context)	*broad* (a theological question in its philosophical and historical context)
length of reflection	*brief* (one or two sessions)	*intermediate* (several weeks or months)	*indeterminate* (complexity of reflection and commitment to insight rather than action; therefore, reflection is viewed as ongoing)
conversation partners	personal and ministerial experience	theology and social sciences as well as experience	philosophy and history
example: Christian community	this community's effort to live its Christian ideals; skills for community building and resolution of problems	this community's experience in explicit relation to the Christian tradition and the surrounding culture	Christian community as interpreted by scriptural images and historical understandings of church; ecclesiology

Figure 1

these two models of reflection is their immediacy and concreteness; the scope of inquiry is narrowed to an immediate concern. An added strength of the first method is its attention to the minister's relationship (emotional and cognitive) to the concern. Weaknesses sometimes experienced in both methods are the lack of explicit attention given to the Christian tradition in regard to this pastoral concern and a difficulty of moving from such concrete incidents to broader theological understanding. Each of these methods has contributed significantly to the development of theological reflection in ministry. Both differ from the academic model of theological reflection discussed previously in immediacy of scope, in the length of the reflection (usually being completed in one or two sessions), and in the conversation partners (giving little attention to either historical or philosophical considerations).

The process of theological reflection elaborated in this book situates itself midway on the ministry-theology continuum. It focuses on a pastoral concern in both its immediate dimension (What is *my* experience of it? What has been its impact on *this* community?) and its broader religious import (How has the Christian tradition responded to this kind of concern?). Thus, the scope of this method is broader than a straightforward reflection on an immediate concern, but more experientially rooted than a reflection in the method of Lonergan or Tracy. These characteristics suggest the kind of minister for whom this model was devised: the minister who is neither exclusively an activist nor a professional theologian; the minister who needs and wants time for reflection in ministry; the minister who wants to be more critically aware of the influence of the Christian tradition, culture, and personal experience on pastoral decision making.

Pastoral Reflection: A Corporate Task

A contemporary shift in ecclesiology, our understanding of the nature and structure of the church, has significantly influenced the shape of theological reflection in ministry. Previously, we have been familiar with denominational structures in which an individual authority (whether Catholic pope, Episcopal bishop, or Baptist pastor) reflected on and made decisions for the believing community. The emphasis today moves toward understanding the community of faith as the locus of theological and pastoral reflection. Pastoral insight and decision are not just received in the community but are generated there as well. Theological reflection becomes a responsibility of the community itself, a corporate task. This shift is evidenced in the recent growth of ministry teams and in the increased involvement of the laity at all levels of Christian life and ministry. This shift requires new pastoral skills—group reflection, conflict resolution, and decision making—for the community and for its ministers.

The method that we discuss here is intended to assist the corporate task of theological reflection. Its development has been itself a corporate endeavor. The model and method were formulated initially over the course of a two-year research project undertaken with the support of the Lilly Endowment. The research group consisted of a biblical scholar (Eugene Ulrich), a ministry educator (Gordon Myers), a social scientist (Evelyn Whitehead), and a theologian (James Whitehead). At the core of the project was a year-long conversation, structured in eight workshop sessions, which engaged ten women and men experienced in ministry in dialogue with the research group. These creative collaborators were: Judith Anne Beattie, Gregory Green, Thomas Jones, John Phalen, Joy O'Grady, Jane Pitz, Mary Anne Roemer, Frank Quinlivan, Michael Rosswurm, and Richard Stieglitz.

Together, the participants explored a series of questions: the nature of Christian vocation and ministry, the contemporary experience of Christian community, the shape of adult religious growth, Christian understandings of sexuality and marriage, the mission of the church in the world. The intent of the dialogue was twofold: to discover how effective ministers do, in fact, reflect on these questions as they arise in their ministry and to describe and further elaborate the process through which persons in ministry reach decisions for pastoral action.

It is our hope that this method of reflection, tested and refined in a variety of settings, will be useful both to Christian ministers and to ministry education. The value of such a practical method will be confirmed, not by its sophistication, but by its effectiveness as a tool of reflective Christian communities in their efforts of ministry and service.

Notes

1. See Paul Tillich's presentation of method in theology in Volume One of his *Systematic Theology* (Chicago: University of Chicago Press, 1951). See also Bernard Lonergan, *Method in Theology* (New York: Herder and Herder, 1972); Elisabeth Schüssler Fiorenza, *In Memory of Her: A Feminist Theological Reconstruction of Christian Origins* (New York: Crossroad, 1983); David Tracy's *Blessed Rage for Order* (New York: Seabury, 1975).

2. See David Tracy's reflection in *Blessed Rage for Order*, p. 49ff.

Method in Ministry

· Part I ·

Theological Reflection in Ministry

A complex and changing world challenges us to discern the continuing presence and action of God and to respond, faithfully and effectively, to this presence. For Christian communities and their ministerial leaders this requires a method of reflection.

Part One outlines a model and method of pastoral reflection. In the tri-polar model we set out three sources of religiously relevant information: our own life experience, the Christian tradition, and the insights and biases of our culture. In the three-stage method we examine the movement from insight to pastoral action: a process of attending, assertion, and response. The goal of this model and method of reflection is to support reflective Christian ministers and communities as their faith finds effective expression in today's world.

· 1 ·

Pastoral Reflection: A Model and a Method

IN EVERY AGE THE COMMUNITY OF FAITH MUST DISCOVER THE SHAPE OF its ministry. We must discern how we are to be faithful to the gospel and effective in our mission: to celebrate God's saving presence and to contribute, by word and action and sacrament, to the fullness of this presence—God's reign that comes in justice and peace. Theological reflection is an essential tool in this discernment of contemporary ministry. The goal of developing a method of reflection in Christian life is not simply to help believers understand more clearly, but to help them to act more effectively—that is, in ways that are faithful to the good news of salvation made known to us in Jesus Christ—and to help them become competent in proclaiming this good news in our own time.

Christians today need a *portable* method: a reflective process that they can carry with them to the daily duties and challenges of their life of faith. We also need a *performable* method: a style of discernment that is simple and straightforward enough to lead our reflections toward practical action. And we need a *communal* method: a shared strategy by which Christian gatherings can face the challenges in their surrounding culture and come to agreement of how to witness to their faith here and now.

Through much of the twentieth century, theologians have described theological method as a correlation of Christian faith and contemporary experience.[1] Paul Tillich cast this correlation as a question of "existential questions and theological answers in mutual interdependence." Shubert Ogden spoke of the relationship as "the correlation of the Christian witness of faith and human existence."

David Tracy described the correlation as the interaction of "common human experience" and "the Christian fact."[2]

But recently the image of theological reflection as correlation has begun to give way to the livelier metaphor of conversation. To some, *correlation* suggests that the interaction of faith and culture proceeds on a cooly rational plane. But when we gather to reflect on the vital implications of our faith, something more robust and less controllable than a "correlation" occurs. *Conversation*, with its possibilities for interruption, disagreement and surprise, seems a more adequate image.

The invigorating exchanges between Christian faith and contemporary life range from dialogue to debate to accusation. And though incivility imperils the conversation, disagreement and misunderstanding are to be expected. Genuine conversation, David Tracy reminds us, has some hard rules:

> Say only what you mean; say it as accurately as you can; listen to and respect what the other says, however different or other; be willing to correct or defend your opinions if challenged by the conversation partner; be willing to argue if necessary, to confront if demanded, to endure necessary conflict, to change your mind if the evidence suggests it.[3]

The metaphor of conversation reminds us that pastoral reflection is meant to be a communal exercise, not a monologue nor a lecture. If only one person's voice is heard or only one group's concerns are acknowledged, there is no conversation. Finally, theological reflection as a conversation is not simply an emergency strategy to meet a momentary need. We do not have a conversation—about poverty or consumerism or sexuality or authority—so that we can settle the matter once and for all and be done with the need for such engagement. The conversation *is* our life together. Such a community dialogue is a habit, both pleasurable and painful, in which our faith is tested and matures. This realization helps us bridge the gap between theological reflection as a specialized discipline and the everyday life of Christian faith.

In this chapter we present both a model and a method for doing theological reflection in ministry. The model points to the participants in the conversation, helping us recognize the different voices and alerting us to their authority. The method shows us how the conversation proceeds—how the different participants in the dialogue present their case, engage one another, and move toward a practical response.

Three conversation partners comprise the model of pastoral reflection presented here. One is Christian tradition: our religious heritage embracing both Sacred Scripture and the long history of the Christian church with its multiple and changing interpretations of the Bible and of its own life.[4]

Who are the tradition's conversation partners? Theologians have commonly identified a single partner in the dialogue: for example, Tracy's "common human experience" or Ogden's "human existence." Our method separates this broad category into two distinct but overlapping sources: experience and culture.

We identify the *experience* of individual Christians and the collective *experience* of faith communities as voices essential to the conversation. In fact, most pastoral reflection begins here, triggered by the hopes and confusions of our own lives. And life experience does more than provoke us to reflect; the wisdom carried in our personal and communal histories illumines the reflection as well. These histories are themselves profoundly influenced by both Christian faith and the surrounding culture. Nevertheless, *experience* merits explicit consideration in pastoral reflection.

The third conversation partner in a theological reflection we name *culture*, designating the convictions, values and biases that form the social setting in which the reflection takes place. Culture in this sense points to the formative symbols and ongoing interpretations that shape our world-view, as well as the social roles and political structures that shape social life.

The *method* of theological reflection describes how the conversation among our religious heritage, our experience, and our cultural life proceeds. This dynamic moves from listening to assertion to pastoral response.[5] The reflective process first carefully attends to relevant information available in each of the three sources, then actively engages this information by bringing the different perspectives into assertive dialogue. These movements of listening and assertion require skill: not only textual and hermeneutical abilities—the theological skills of attending, but interpersonal abilities—the skills to listen well to other people's experience and insight.

Assertion requires a similar breadth, as pastoral reflection sustains the tension of differing interpretations not only among participants but in Scripture and tradition as well. Out of such assertively maintained tensions, theological insight and pastoral decisions begin to emerge. The final stage of the method, then, is intimately related to and flows from the prior stages of attending and assertion. We will examine this three-step movement in greater detail after exploring the *model* of theological reflection.

The Model

Theological reflection in ministry instigates a conversation among three sources of religiously relevant information—the experience of the community of faith, the Christian tradition, and the resources of the culture.

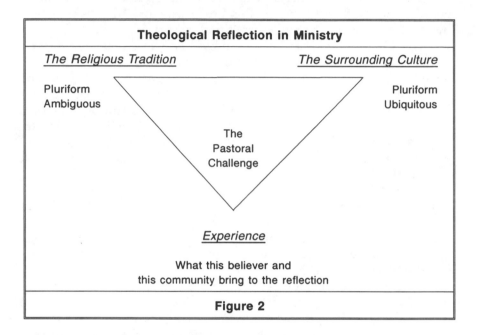

Figure 2

1. Religious Tradition

Our religious heritage brings to the dialogue the massive range of insight and grace that Scripture and Christian history have given us. *Tradition* for Christians spans the beliefs and convictions imbedded not only in Scripture and the church councils at Nicaea and Chalcedon but in denominational history as well, with its theological statements and pastoral guidelines. When we face a particular ministry concern, we turn instinctively to these sources to guide our response.

Confronting this daunting source of religious information called tradition brings us face-to-face with questions about its force in our life and the nature of religious revelation. Many Christians have grown up with an image of our scriptural tradition as absolute and ahistorical. We understood the Bible as God's revelation coming to us directly, without the interference of human involvement. The paramount value of our scriptural tradition was that it transcended experience and so was *not* tainted by the vicissitudes of human society. This ahistorical vision of God's presence in human history gave our Scripture and our sacred history a patina of absolute certitude. The Bible, it seemed to us, held constant and clear answers to thorny contemporary questions.

Recent biblical scholarship has brought Christians to a richer realization: Our sacred texts themselves originated in a people's experience, our religious ancestors' encounters with the mystery of God. These experiences—of burning bushes, of rescue from exile, of Christ recognized in the stranger at Emmaus—were collected first as oral history, then preserved in written texts. The spoken and written words that handed on these profound religious experiences were necessarily "cultural words"—words imbedded in and carrying the limits of a particular culture.

Christian tradition brings to the conversation not ahistorical truths but compelling glimpses of God's mysterious presence in our past and present. Our religious heritage contributes to the conversation of contemporary faith not sound-bites of salvation but privileged metaphors. These metaphors—God's lasting covenant, our stewardship in creation, the paradox of the cross—illumine our journey of faith. They hint of a plot hidden in the mayhem of human history; they offer trustworthy scripts to follow—scripts of generosity and self-sacrifice, of justice and charity—as we struggle to make sense of our personal and shared lives.

The Tradition as Pluriform

The Christian tradition has been pluriform from its inception. Diversity is apparent in the earliest faith communities, with the church at Antioch formulating a Christology somewhat different from that of Corinth. In the New Testament itself there are four gospel accounts, not one. Each attempts to express the mystery of God's gift to us in Jesus, but their interpretations differ. Warning that "the world" is a threat to faith, for example, the Fourth Gospel suggests that salvation is *from* the world. Jesus is remembered saying, "I have chosen you out of the world; therefore the world hates you (John 15:19)." The accounts of the other three gospels argue that the world is the very site of our salvation; here Jesus tells his disciples repeatedly that the kingdom of God is breaking into their world here and now.

The dazzling pluriformity of our religious heritage, so familiar to the professional theologian, remains a source of confusion for many believers. The method of reflection we discuss here assumes an understanding of Christian pluralism not only as scandal and sign of disunity (which it has been), but also as a sign of richness. The variety of expressions of belief within the Christian tradition points to the ineffably diverse ways God is with us. As an educational tool, this model of pastoral reflection attempts to develop a greater awareness of and an increased comfort with this pluriformity.

Diverse in its beginnings, the tradition is pluriform over its long history as well. As the heritage of Christianity unfolded, new voices were heard: Augustine of Hippo, Hildegard of Bingen, Martin Luther, Martin Luther King. These voices, speaking out of novel cultural contexts, helped rephrase our faith, bringing out nuances previously unnoticed.[6]

Historically, the tradition has developed as Christianity interacted (with varying effectiveness and faithfulness) with different cultural contexts and challenges. This historical movement results in a religious heritage rich with responses to particular pastoral concerns. Recognizing this historical pluriformity helps faith communities today appreciate more clearly the tradition's flexibility and breadth.

The complex saga of Christian tradition is diverse in yet another way. Christians have traditionally acknowledged this third pluriformity by recognizing the church as both human and divine. In more contemporary imagery we recognize that every religious heritage carries a history of both grace and malpractice. The tradition hands on extraordinary gifts and insights; through it God's grace and healing have touched generations of believers. This same heritage carries and hands on grievous wounds. The malpractice of Christian history is part of our religious inheritance. Denying this legacy of personal and institutional failure leaves our faith naive and, ultimately, incredible. But when we are overwhelmed by our past's woundedness we forget the evidence of God's persistent grace, through which the church survives the sins of our ancestors and our own worst failings.

Religious leaders are often hesitant to admit this history of malpractice "lest the faithful be scandalized." But, paradoxically, grappling with the institution's historical and current frailties often results in a deeper appreciation of the tradition's vitality and gifts. Listening to the varied voices of our religious heritage, the goal is to recover and to overcome.[7] We struggle to recover the saving words and healing insights of our shared past, even as we attempt to overcome the bias and distortion that still infect our common life. The graces and wounds of our religious tradition give reflective Christians an enduring agenda of both thanksgiving and healing.

Befriending the Tradition

How do the reflective community and its ministers relate to this source in pastoral reflection? The riches of the Christian heritage, ironically, remain unavailable to many in ministry. In our experience, pastoral ministers often feel alienated from the tradition. This is not an emotional alienation or rejection of what the tradition holds. It is, rather, a pervasive sense of *distance*. Most in ministry display great respect for their religious heritage yet frequently feel intimidated by its weight. Formal preparation for ministry has given them an appreciation of the complexity and sacredness of the tradition, but not the skills of access that are appropriate to their own profession.[8]

For their part, parishioners faced with a personal crisis or social concern often see the religious heritage as narrowly judgmental, or unhelpfully ambiguous, or simply irrelevant. Ministers and faithful alike sense they lack both the tools and the time to engage the tradition as a resource for practical decision making. Thus, a challenge for theological reflection in ministry is to develop methods of access to the tradition that are appropriate not to the scripture scholar or systematic theologian, but to those working directly within the community of faith. For both minister and faithful, the goal is not mastery but befriending—an increase in intimacy with the tradition.[9] The image of *befriending* suggests a more-than-intellectual grasp, a familiarity that includes both appreciative awareness of the tradition and comfort with its diversity and contradictions.

2. Experience

In this model, the voice of our religious heritage enjoys a privileged position but another voice instigates the conversation. Pastoral reflection begins as we confront an urgent concern, a pressing issue arising in personal or communal experience. Starting a reflection in experience seems obvious, but this voice has not always been heard in the theological conversation. Another logic recommends "beginning at the beginning," with biblical texts or church teachings, and working forward. Practically, such a reflection frequently fails to come to terms with experience. So our method begins in experience, acknowledging the perils of this starting point.

Beginning in experience risks becoming bogged down in narrow self-interest or being swept away by self-deception. To be cautious of authoritative claims made by single individuals makes sense, especially in the U.S. culture where the tabloid press and talk-show hosts exalt personal experience, the more outrageous the better.

The challenge of this practical method is to assist the minister and the community to come to a reflective grasp of their own experience (convictions, feelings, ideas, biases) about a specific pastoral concern. As theologians Patricia Killen and John de Beer remind us, "when we enter our experience—narrate it non-judgmentally and attentively—we find it saturated with feeling."[10] Most of us have difficulty acknowledging these feelings and tracing the experiences that give rise to them. To understand our experience we need skills of awareness and listening. So developing those skills that enable faith communities to attend critically to this most immediate and potentially volatile source of religiously significant information is imperative.

In the workshops in which this model of theological reflection was developed, a variety of experiential learning strategies were used to help participants explore their experience and conviction concerning specific ministerial questions. For example, journal keeping, exercises of the imagination, and structured small group sessions were methods employed to approach deeper levels of personal and professional experience. The intention of this stage of the method is that self-knowledge which has always been a central part of Christian spirituality. As believers come to greater consciousness and clarity about their personal feelings and convictions on a particular pastoral question, this experience can be placed in an assertive conversation with insights drawn from Christian tradition and the culture.

The Sense of the Faithful: Where Tradition and Experience Meet

At first glance the venerable religious heritage and our fragile experience seem far apart. But these two conversation partners come together in the ancient Christian notion of "the sense of the faithful" *(sensus fidelium)*. As believers struggle to be faithful to their past, they respond in ways that register a contemporary fidelity to this heritage. Contemporary experience and Christian tradition embrace. In fact, a religious heritage only survives by being engaged and embraced in each new generation.

The Second Vatican Council reminded Catholics of the rich potential of "the sense of the faithful." In the document on the church *(Lumen Gentium)* the bishops first described this instinctual grasp of faith in terms of a universal and error-free agreement:

> Thanks to a supernatural sense of faith which characterizes the People as a whole, it manifests this unerring quality when 'from the bishops down to the last member of the laity,' it shows universal agreement in matters of faith and morals.[11]

Later this vision of a largely passive sense of faith expands to include a more lively and active edge: the sense of faith "clings without fail to the faith once delivered to the Saints, penetrates it more deeply by accurate insights, and applies it more thoroughly to life." These energetic verbs—*clings, penetrates, applies*—describe the activities of lively communities engaging their faith in response to contemporary demands.

As a reflective community examines its experience on a pastoral question, it will recognize attitudes that betray an imbeddedness in its culture. The consumerism of United States culture, for example, or its "can do" activist bias quickly become apparent. Reflection also reveals aspects of our experience that find their origins in unique personal histories—the strengths and wounds inherited from one's family and ethnic background. But communal reflection also uncovers how significantly our feelings and convictions have been shaped by our experience of faith, how fruitful have been our often-failing efforts to "put on Christ." Here the sense of the faithful finds its most concrete expression.

The *sensus fidelium* represents the overlap of tradition and experience, reminding us that in the Christian community these conversation partners converge. Pastoral reflection helps the faith community recognize where its gathered experience and its religious inheritance come together. This tested awareness becomes the ground and warrant for its active witness of faith, not only to the larger society but within the church as well. The *sensus fidelium* reminds the local church that it is more than a passive receptacle of the truths of its religious past. Fidelity requires not only that the faith community *cling to* what it has received; it demands the courage to *penetrate* this ongoing experience of faith anew and the audacity to *apply* its new awareness in contemporary life. This continuing penetration and application is the substance of theological reflection in ministry.[12]

3. Cultural Resources

The third partner in the conversation that is theological reflection in ministry we identify as *culture*. Here we examine the attitudes, values and biases that constitute the social milieu in which we live. Culture's pervasiveness and invisibility challenge pastoral reflection from the start. Our own culture surrounds us like the air we breathe; it is so ordinary and natural that we seldom notice its influence.

Cultural forces that are ancient or alien are easier to recognize. Church historians, for example, describe the influence of the second and third century stoic philosophy on the Christian vision of the

human passions.[13] Stoicism's harsh judgment of anger and grief and
sexual passion profoundly shaped Christian spirituality, even down
to our own time. Living in a culture that carries different interpretations of emotional life helps us see stoicism's earlier influence. But
tracking how our own culture shapes our emotional lives remains
difficult.

As a conversation partner in pastoral reflection, culture speaks
in many voices. Some of these influential voices are more readily
recognized: the violence portrayed in popular film and television;
the prevalence of prejudice; the constant pressure of advertising in a
consumer economy. Communal reflection on contemporary Christian life will be alert to these often insidious influences.

But culture speaks in other voices, some of which strengthen
the community's discernment. Consider the contribution of the social sciences to an understanding of the person and society. In the
workshops in which this model of reflection was initially developed,
for example, information from the social sciences played a central
role. The potential contributions of psychological theories of adult
maturation to a contemporary Christian spirituality were probed and
sociological perspectives on community were examined for insight
into the hopes and challenges of Christian life together.

The voices of culture, then, speak with both positive and negative force. Neither simply demonic nor unambiguously enlightened,
culture produces interpretations which the Christian tradition rejects
and also provides interpretations which challenge Christian reflection to reconsider and correct limitations within its own self-understanding. Sexuality provides a good example of this ambiguity.
Christians struggle against the influence of pornography in society,
but benefit from the contributions of medical and psychological research to a clearer understanding of mature sexuality. The pole of
cultural information thus represents not a realm of unredeemed nature, but a mixed environment, partly antithetical to and partly complementary to Christian life.

Here again, access is an important concern: how to make information from social and cultural sources available in the reflective community? The minister cannot be asked to become either a philosopher or
social scientist. Instead, we must continue to explore ways—both
practical and critical—to bring culture's perspective and information
into the conversation that is pastoral reflection.

The Method

A faith community gathers to reflect on some important aspect of its shared life. A question of personal ethics or public life bewilders us. How are we to respond? What does God want of us here?

The *model* of theological reflection offers a way to structure our conversation, paying attention to three sources of information: our cultural setting, our religious heritage, and our own special experience about this question. The *method* of reflection suggests a process by which we pursue this communal discernment. Beginning in listening, the method moves us to assertion and then toward practical pastoral response.

Three-Stage Method of Theological Reflection in Ministry

1. **Attending**
Seeking out the information on a particular pastoral concern that is available in personal experience, Christian tradition, and cultural resources. Listening critically while suspending judgment.

2. **Assertion**
Bringing the perspectives gathered from these three sources into a lively dialogue of mutual clarification to expand and enrich religious insight. Having the courage to share our convictions and the willingness to be challenged.

3. **Pastoral Response**
Moving from discussion and insight to decision and action. Discerning how to respond; planning what to do; evaluating how we have done.

Figure 3

---

1. Attending

"Let anyone with ears, listen!" (Matthew 11:15) The initial posture for theological reflection is that of the listener; attending is the first activity of the method. Faced with a particular concern, the reflective community seeks out the information that is available in their experience, in the religious tradition and in the surrounding culture. But this gospel command reminds us that hearing is neither automatic nor easy.

A range of listening skills is required of us if we are to discern what is happening among us and what God would have us do. Benefiting from recent biblical scholarship, ministers and other

Christians have become more skillful at listening to the texts and
contexts of Christian Scripture. As believers, they also approach
Scripture as a religious resource that can influence their personal
lives and inform their practical ministerial decisions.

Other listening skills pertinent to the other sources of information described in the model are needed. To attend to experience as a
source in theological reflection requires skillful behavior. Skills of
introspection alert us to the movements of our own mind and heart,
helping us become aware of personal motives, biases, convictions
and values. This self-awareness is an essential part of spiritual
growth; it is also critical to any process of pastoral reflection.

Other disciplines help us listen in community. In the midst of
an important meeting, for example, participants often find themselves ignoring other people while they internally rehearse their own
next comment. Or fatigue or anxiety in a group distract members
from what other people have to contribute. We recognize here that
listening is more than a personal skill. Groups need to devise ways
to hold themselves attentive to new information both from within
and beyond their own membership.

Developing the disciplines of listening reminds religious leaders that their role is not only to direct the community of faith but to
learn from it. A faith community is not merely the passive recipient
of religious truth but an active setting of faith. As part of the *sensus
fidelium*, this community has a contribution to make to the church's
ongoing self-understanding, a contribution that is possible only as
ministers and theologians listen carefully and expectantly to this
source. Listening skills are required, too, as religious leaders approach cultural sources. While ministers cannot be expected to develop the skills of professional social scientists, some critical openness to learn from the culture is imperative in their leadership role.

A necessary ingredient in effective listening to each of these
sources is the ability to suspend premature judgment. Suspending
judgment is, of course, a threatening venture. Opening ourselves to
new information leaves us vulnerable to challenge and even to
change. Yet the effectiveness of this first stage of theological reflection depends on the ability to explore honestly the information available in the three sources. A tendency to quick evaluation will cut
short this exploration and lessen the chance of coming to new insight
that may lead to creative pastoral response.

2. Assertion

All three sources of information described in the model contribute to theological reflection in ministry. The contribution of each is

not made in isolation, but in an assertive relationship of challenge and confirmation. Two assumptions ground this conviction: (1) God is revealed in all three sources and (2) the religious information available in each source is partial. While the limitation of personal experience and cultural information as religious resources may be more immediately evident, there are limitations to be recognized in the tradition as well—limitations that arise from the human interpretations and cultural contexts that have shaped the tradition. Culturally rooted biases *for* hierarchical models of leadership in the church today and *against* equal access of women to positions of ministerial leadership show such limitations. Our faithful efforts to both recover and overcome our religious past are facilitated by placing the tradition's insights on a pastoral concern in assertive dialogue with the community's experience and with cultural information. It is in this dialogue of mutual interpretation that new insight is generated and the shape of pastoral response begins to emerge.

This second stage in the method can be clarified in two metaphors. The first, as we have noted, is *conversation*: the different voices that we have heard in the attending stage are now allowed to *speak to* one another. The challenge here is to bring these separate and often conflicting voices into contact. The second image is a *crucible*: the diverse information is poured into a single container, where insights and convictions are allowed to interact with one another. A crucible suggests the transformation that often occurs at this stage—if we handle the volatile components with care.

Assertive engagement is a style of behavior which acknowledges the value of one's own needs and convictions in a manner that respects the needs and convictions of others. Assertive behavior functions between the extremes of not being able to express personal convictions (non-assertiveness) and forcing one's convictions on others (aggressiveness). In the metaphor of conversation, the overly assertive person dominates the discussion; the insufficiently assertive person withdraws and does not participate. In both instances, the communal effort is defeated.

A theological reflection is aborted when either nonassertiveness or aggressiveness predominates. This can happen in a variety of ways. A member of the community may become so absorbed in personal experience as to be deaf to the voice of the religious heritage. Here experience is an aggressor, frustrating the conversation. Likewise, a person may be so overwhelmed by an interpretation in the tradition that he or she is closed to cultural insight or even to the testimony of personal experience. Here, the tradition (or, more precisely, one interpretation of an aspect of the tradition) is an aggressor in the reflection. Or a person may be so impressed by a cultural interpretation that the religious perspective appears utterly irrelevant. Here again the conversation stalls, defeated by a failure to establish a genuinely assertive relationship among the three sources of information.

Pastoral reflection requires assertion at both a theological and an interpersonal level. A willingness to face diversity and to tolerate ambiguity are essential. With these, a faith community can sustain different and possibly conflicting testimony about a single issue. This model of reflection argues that only with the mature development of this stage of mutual assertion can the reflective process move toward the final stage of pastoral response.

3. Pastoral Response

The information gained by listening we bring into the interplay of assertion, with the hope that this dynamic interaction will generate insight on how we should respond. The challenge of the third movement of the method is to translate insight into action. The effectiveness of this stage depends on the quality of the earlier reflection. The choices available to the community now arise from insights clarified in the assertion stage. Integral pastoral decisions are expressive of and in continuity with these insights.

Here a crucial difference between theological decisions and ministerial decisions becomes more apparent. The minister reflects in order to act. In the face of insufficient information or conflicting facts, a reflection accountable only to the criteria of academic theology can decide not to decide. Instead the theologian can, appropriately, reinitiate the process of reflection in the hope of coming to greater clarity sometime in the future. A ministerial reflection most generally focuses on a question that demands practical resolution now. In many situations the community must act even in the face of partial information. Pastoral reflection which takes as its criteria those standards of clarity and comprehensiveness appropriate in academic theological reflection will necessarily fall short of practical usefulness.

The decision stage begins by focussing the best insights of the assertion stage. What is our response to be to these communal convictions, now clarified and confirmed? In this *particular* situation, what are we to do? Sometimes the fruit of pastoral reflection is change, even significant transformation. Sometimes an established policy or familiar practice is re-affirmed, now at a deeper level of commitment. Frequently reflection leads us to courageous action. But in moments of profound loss—or joy—we may be led deeper into mystery. Confronted by God's ways that overturn our expectations and defy our puny efforts at control, we pray instead for patience: "teach us to sit still . . . even among these rocks." Action may follow later, but our present discipline is reverent waiting on the Lord.

Theological reflection in ministry fails when pastoral decisions ignore the communities in which they will be implemented. Thus, consensus building—the ability to move from honored diversity to shared action—becomes a skill of pastoral reflection. Tools of problem analysis and conflict resolution help a community bring the force of their reflection to bear on group decisions. Strategies of group decision making assist this transition from insight to action. Central to these are the ability to generate alternatives, to choose among these partial solutions, and to keep these choices accountable to the larger vision of the reign of God.

Conclusion

A goal of Christian ministry is the formation of reflective communities alive to the presence of God. The model that we suggest here can serve as a tool, inviting believers to develop skills enabling them to discern religiously significant information in three important sources. Such a community is attentive to the normative heritage of the tradition and sensitive to its cultural milieu and to its own experience of faith. Aware that, as a single group, it is not the sole arbiter of faith, the community is yet confident as it shares its convictions within the church. These convictions will be expressed in pastoral decisions that are at once practical and open to revision, as the community continues to attend to convictions that arise in other faith communities.

In a church that is genuinely catholic, different communities will come to differing conclusions in many concrete pastoral situations. Some of these differences may arise from ignorance or error or even "bad will." More often, however, these differences will be appropriate and expectable variations that reflect the rich diversity within the Christian experience of God's Word and God's will.

Notes

1. Francis Schüssler Fiorenza provides a brief, clear summary of the method of correlation in theology in "Systematic Theology: Tasks and Methods" in *Systematic Theology: Roman Catholic Perspectives*, Vol. I, edited by Francis Schüssler Fiorenza and John P. Galvin (Minneapolis: Fortress, 1991), pp. 55-61. Anne Carr outlines the influences of feminist theologians on methods of theological reflection in "The New Vision of Feminist Theology," pp. 5-29 in *Freeing Theology: The Essentials of Theology in Feminist Per-*

spective, edited by Catherine Mowry LaCugna (HarperSanFrancisco, 1993). The work that most influenced the first edition of *Method in Ministry* was David Tracy's *Blessed Rage for Order* (New York: Seabury, 1975). Also influential was Bernard Lonergan's *Method in Theology* (New York: Herder & Herder, 1972).

2. See Paul Tillich's *Systematic Theology* (Chicago: University of Chicago Press, 1951), Vol. I, p. 60; Shubert Ogden's "What is Theology?", *Journal of Religion* 52 (January 1972), p. 23 and David Tracy's *Blessed Rage for Order*, p. 43.

3. David Tracy, *Plurality and Ambiguity* (San Francisco: Harper & Row, 1987), p. 19.

4. Lewis Mudge discusses the content and process of the Christian tradition in an aptly named section, "The Travail of Tradition," in his *The Sense of a People: Toward a Church for the Human Future* (Philadelphia, PA: Trinity Press International, 1992), p. 63 ff. Also see Edward Farley's discussion of the tradition as "a house of authority" in his *Ecclesial Reflection: An Anatomy of Theological Method* (Philadelphia, PA: Fortress Press, 1982), p. 101 ff. For a comprehensive view of tradition see Yves Congar's *The Meaning of Tradition*, Section 1, Vol. 3 of *Twentieth Century Encyclopedia of Catholicism* (New York: Hawthorn, 1964), and sociologist Edward Shils' *Tradition* (Chicago, IL: University of Chicago Press, 1981).

5. Bernard Lonergan's theological method, in a parallel movement, extends through four stages: experience; understanding (of its meaning); assessment (of its value); decision. See Francis Schüssler Fiorenza's summary of this complex method in his article on systematic theology noted above.

6. Avery Dulles reminds Catholics that their tradition is more than a body of teachings. The Second Vatican Council tried to recapture the vitality and fluidity of our religious heritage, teaching that "this tradition which comes from the apostles progresses in the Church with the help of the Holy Spirit"(*Dei Verbum*, 8); See Dulles' chapter on faith and revelation in *Systematic Theology: Roman Catholic Perspectives*, eds. Francis Schüssler Fiorenza and John P. Galvin (Minneapolis, MN: Fortress Press, 1991), Vol. I, p. 89-128; we quote here from p. 121.

7. Karl Rahner makes this distinction in his "Current Problems in Christology," in *Theological Investigations* (Baltimore, MD: Helicon, 1961), Vol. I, pp. 149-54.

8. Robert L. Kinast, in both his written work and his consultant ministry through the Center for Theological Reflection (P.O. Box 726, Indian Rocks Beach, FL 34635), provides valuable resources for doing theological reflection in the context of ministry and ministry education. See his *Let the Ministry Teach: A Handbook for Theological Reflection* (Center for Theological Reflection, 1992) and *If Only You Recognized God's Gift: John's Gospel as an Illustration of Theological Reflection* (Grand Rapids, MI: William Eerdmans, 1993).

9. Thomas Groome's influential work on "shared praxis" gives ministers and religious educators both a compelling vision and practical strategies for opening the resources of the tradition to the faith community; see his *Christian Religious Education: Sharing Our Story and Vision* (San Francisco: Harper & Row, 1980) and *Sharing Faith: A Comprehensive Approach to Religious Education and Pastoral Ministry* (San Francisco: Harper & Row, 1991).

10. Patricia O'Connell Killen and John de Beer, *The Art of Theological Reflection* (New York: Crossroad, 1994), p. 27.

11. The Second Vatican Council discussed the *sensus fidelium* in "The Dogmatic Constitution on the Church," *Lumen Gentium*, Paragraph 12 in *The Documents of Vatican II*, edited by Walter M. Abbott (New York: America Press, 1966), pp. 29-30.

12. For the on-going discussion of this elusive notion, see Avery Dulles' "Sensus Fidelium," *America* (Nov. 1, 1986), pp. 240-43 and Edmund Dobbins' "Sensus Fidelium Reconsidered," in *New Theology Review*, 2 (August, 1989), pp. 48-65. In "The Seasoning of Senses" we explore ways to help a community recognize and honor its sense of faith; see our *Seasons of Strength* (Winona, MN: Saint Mary's Press, 1995), Chapter 5.

13. See Peter Brown's excellent study *The Body and Society: Men, Women, and Sexual Renunciation in Early Christianity* (New York: Columbia University Press, 1988).

• Part II •

The Model of Reflection in Ministry

Each of the three sources of religiously relevant information to which the reflective Christian must attend is complex and plural.

The Christian tradition comprises not only the Old and New Testaments, but the two millennia of interpretations and decisions that have shaped Christian history. The minister's approach to this rich and dense heritage is not one of mastery, but of befriending.

The community's own lived experience, another source of information, is both shaped and challenged by this religious heritage and by its cultural milieu. Of central importance in a critical appreciation of this source of information is the question of access: How are we to clarify our own insights and biases as these are a part of our reflection and decision?

Cultural information, a third source of information, is likewise ambiguous. Literature, philosophy, and the social sciences can contribute positively to our religious understanding of life; other aspects of cultural life—class discrimination, materialism, environmental neglect—can influence our awareness in a destructive fashion.

In Part Two we explore the complexity of each of these sources in terms of their contribution to theological reflection in ministry.

The Tradition in Theological Reflection: Scripture and the Minister

Eugene C. Ulrich and
William G. Thompson

THE CONVERSATION THAT IS CHRISTIAN TRADITION BRINGS TO PASTORAL reflection the Judeo-Christian memory of God's saving presence among us. These recollections have been recorded in various languages and transmitted through different cultures. The privileged experiences of our tradition survive today in liturgical rituals, theological doctrines and daily piety. The retelling of these stories of salvation has been, at different times, compromised by the biases of both story teller and community. This vast array of insight, grace and bias we inherit as our religious tradition.[1]

In this chapter we examine only the critical core of this long tradition—the Hebrew and Christian Scriptures. We explore the function of this most authoritative part of our tradition in theological reflection—conscious that "Scripture is itself a product of tradition."[2] We will describe a way of approaching the Bible that attends to tradition, uses cultural information and respects personal experience. Our aim is to elaborate an approach that is theologically rooted and genuinely available to persons in ministry.

Christian theologians in every age have acknowledged the biblical writings as a norm for Christian theology. In ministry education, a central question is how the church is to use the Bible in its practice of prayer, in its preaching, in its liturgical life, and in its theology. In this chapter we approach the Bible from this viewpoint of faith. We ask how Scripture functions in pastoral reflection and how the biblical tradition can come alive for the community engaged in such reflection.

Many persons in ministry today have come to the honest but disconcerting realization that their day-to-day pastoral activities often seem separate from Scripture and tradition. They see the need and the value of incorporating Scripture and tradition more explicitly into what they do as ministers. But *how* to do this is not clear.

In their preparation for ministry, religious leaders become aware of the immense complexity of biblical scholarship and Christian history. Their education also awakens an appreciation of the importance of the resources of the Christian heritage, instilling a genuine love for their religious roots. But since ministry students are generally educated by scholars whose tools of inquiry and criteria of effectiveness pertain more to academic theology than to pastoral reflection in ministry, many do not acquire skills that provide access to the tradition at a level appropriate to their ecclesial profession.

Once they are energetically involved in pastoral work, ministers can begin to lose touch with the attitudes and convictions that permeated their seminary education. How can persons whose hours and weeks are filled with the demands and responsibilities of ministry keep abreast of the developments in biblical scholarship? How can they make this information relevant to the people they serve? For many in ministry Scripture continues as a profound resource for personal piety. But its relevance as a resource in one's ministry becomes clouded. What *should* be the function of the Bible in relation to one's ministry? Is there a realistic way to bring Scripture to bear on actual pastoral concerns? How can its power be released in the daily tasks of ministry? We turn to these questions now, first examining *what* the Christian Scriptures are and, then, *how* these central resources of the tradition can be used in reflection in ministry.

Christian Scripture may at times appear distant and alien to the contemporary believer. Set in very different times and cultural contexts, the biblical writings have attained an authority as revelation that creates further distance. In truth, as contemporary scholars remind us, these foundational texts have been discerned and recorded gradually within the experience of believing communities.

In the next section we will examine several of these privileged texts in greater detail. Among the many recorded accounts of the Israelites and the first Christians, only a portion became, in time, "canonized"—gathered into the canon of sacred texts which Christians name the Old and New Testaments.

Recognizing Scripture and tradition as rooted in experience does not reduce the Bible to the status of a poetic history text. We continue to affirm these accounts as the core revelation for Christians, even as we recognize the events they record are not so distant from our own lives. In both Scripture and tradition, faith recognizes human experience shaped by God's presence.

If the Christian Scriptures are, in fact, recordings of and reflections on privileged revelatory experiences, it is also useful to recall the historical processes through which these recordings were collected and passed on from believing community to believing community.

The Composition of the Scriptures

In the following examples, that of the Fourth Gospel and the story of the Exodus, we will elaborate the plural stages and participants in the historical development of these two parts of Scripture. The text of John's Gospel, for example, was not composed in the same way a modern author composes a book. The text whose final written form lies before us today is the last of a series of multiple editions which developed through at least three distinct stages.

First, at the historical stage, Jesus' life included many sayings and actions. Second, at the preaching stage, Jesus' disciples later proclaimed his sayings and deeds in the light of their post-resurrection faith. Third, at the writing stage, the evangelists wrote down in continuous narrative the traditional teachings about Jesus which had developed in oral and written units and collections. At each stage the material was adapted: Jesus adapted "himself to the mentality of his listeners"; the disciples "took into account the needs and circumstances of their listeners"; and the evangelists "adapted what they narrated to the situation of their readers and to the purpose they themselves had in mind."[3]

In the composition of the Gospel of John, then, from sometime after Jesus' death and resurrection to about 100 A.D., a dynamic interaction took place which involved the traditions about Jesus received from the past, the present reflection and experience of John and his disciples, and the lived experience of the communities to which they belonged.[4] Through this interaction, both oral and written, the text was shaped and reshaped through multiple editions until it reached the form in which we now possess it.

Thus, the culmination of God's self-revelation took the concrete form of Jesus' historical life, interpreted and transmitted through the disciples' and evangelists' formulations, all of which was adapted to the historical and theological categories of those to whom the revela-

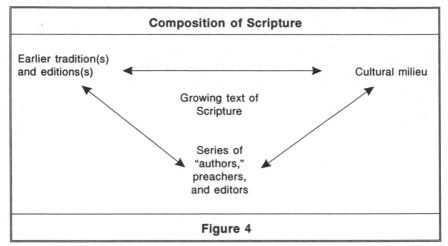

Figure 4

tion was addressed. The point to stress is that this is a *process* and that the process of the development of Scripture is dialectical—*Scripture, which began as experience, was produced through a process of tradition(s) being formulated about that experience and being reformulated by interpreters in dialogue with the experience of their communities and with the larger culture.* The diagram in Figure 4, schematizing the composition of Scripture, is thus not only congruent with, but fundamentally gives rise to, the schema suggested in Chapter One as a model for theological reflection.

A similar dynamic of composition can be seen in the centrally important and plural accounts of the Exodus. The Exodus is the primary foundational event for the religion of Israel, and it is the biblical prototype of saving redemption through Christ.[5] An event in the experience of our cultural ancestors, it was a historical event,[6] the nucleus of which was some sort of historical escape from the Egyptian kingdom by a band of slaves.

The details in the classical text of Exodus we read today are not "eye-witness descriptions of what really happened." It would be strange for slaves fleeing through the desert to find time to compose a written account of their escape. Not written down by Moses or any of the participants, neither was it, understandably, preserved in Egyptian records. Rather, there was a long series of steps between that historical event and the multi-layered text in our present Bible. An analysis of the composition and development of this central text will illumine the inner workings of our scriptural tradition.

The "raw event" of the escape elicited a variety of perceptions by the participants; these perceptions generated different interpretations. Obviously, the Egyptians interpreted and articulated the event differently from the escapees, and the escapees presumably differed among themselves in their interpretations and articulations—from "lucky break" to "our God saved us."[7]

Historical critics would be wary of saying that any of these stages thus far, other than the nucleus of the raw event itself and the final testimony that "God saved us," can be confidently isolated in the text of Exodus. But later, some of the articulations were considered more appropriate and were retold as the *"classic retelling(s)"* of the story. The classic retelling(s) were taken and, with whatever adaptations deemed necessary, incorporated into the larger tapestry of *national narrative traditions*, the oral epic and the written Yahwist and Elohist accounts.[8] In *ritual celebrations* commemorating that saving act by their God, anonymous individuals would celebrate the event in *lyric poetry*:

> *Sing to the* LORD, *for he is gloriously triumphant;*
> *horse and chariot he has cast into the sea* (Exod. 15:21).

This poetic fragment, "The Song of Miriam," is considered to be perhaps the oldest element of the present Exodus narrative. But it is clear that the lyric enthusiasm has adopted an Israelite, not Egyptian, interpretation of the event and shifted from indirect to direct causality. That is, whereas natural forces caused the overthrow of the pursuing Egyptians (see the prose accounts below), the poem looks behind the forces of nature to the God who used those forces as means.

In a *separate hymn*, the "Song of Moses" (Exod. 15:1-18) from the period of the Judges (twelfth to eleventh centuries B.C.), different imagery is used:

> A blast from your nostrils and the waters piled high. . . .

> One breath of yours you blew, and the sea closed over them;
> they sank like lead in the terrible waters.

> . . . you stretched your right hand out, the earth swallowed
> them! (Exod. 15:8, 10, 12)

In yet another retelling, the tenth-century B.C. *Yahwist's narrative*, "Yahweh drove back the sea with a strong easterly wind all night," making "dry land of the sea," and "threw the army into confusion" (Exod. 14:21, 24).

In contrast to the Yahwist's pillar of cloud (14:19b), the ninth-century *Elohist* tells of an "angel of Yahweh, who marched at the front of the army of Israel" (14:19a). Finally, the sixth-century *Priestly Writer* (whose imagery predominates in Hollywood tastes) has Moses lift his rod and divide the sea, the waters being "walls of water to right and to left of them" (14:16, 22).

Thus, there are at least five different voices from across the centuries retelling the escape in differing sets of imagery.[9] Attempts at harmonizing the conflicting details prove to be misguided hyperliteralism. The different "authors" are not intending to describe factual details of what we would call "what really happened." Only two descriptions date within even two centuries of the event, and they are lyrically intent upon pointing out not natural details, but only that it was God who purposefully caused whatever it was that happened.[10]

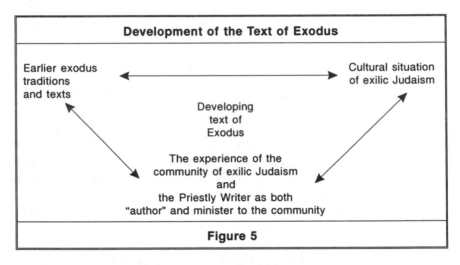

Development of the Text of Exodus

Earlier exodus traditions and texts

Cultural situation of exilic Judaism

Developing text of Exodus

The experience of the community of exilic Judaism and the Priestly Writer as both "author" and minister to the community

Figure 5

The exodus *began in human experience* but was not limited to raw, unreflective experience. It was human experience recognized in faith as shaped by God's presence and purpose. That is, it was *interpreted and formulated in traditional religious categories*, and it was told and retold, shaped and reshaped, in light of the developing needs, the changing cultural situation and worldviews of the successive believing *communities*. A cross-section of the compositional development of the Exodus narrative at the time of the Priestly Writer, its last major contributor, can be seen in Figure 5.

We have emphasized in this chapter Sacred Scripture as grounded in human experience and as plural in its accounts of God's actions among us. The enormous advance in biblical scholarship has taught us, as theologians and ministers, to attend more thoroughly to the plural cultural and historical contexts in which Christian revelation has occurred and been recorded. We have also learned not simply to search out individual biblical passages as proofs of our own theological convictions. Scripture does not serve the contemporary community of faith by providing specific solutions to contemporary questions. In the face of this realization, ministers must learn new modes of faithful and effective access to this central source of revelation and Christian wisdom.

The Use of Scripture in Reflection in Ministry

With this understanding of Scripture, how is the minister to approach it? How does the Bible function, theoretically and practically, in a reflection in ministry? The Scriptures offer us privileged metaphors or, in James Gustafson's vocabulary, "paradigms"[11] that can inform, influence, and inspire us as we approach pastoral issues.

Once produced in their historical contexts, the biblical texts assumed a life of their own and began to function as "paradigms," as they were read and reread in different life situations. When, for example, the Gospel of John won its place in the Christian canon of Scripture, it began to be read and interpreted in relation to Mark, Matthew, and Luke, as well as to the other Old and New Testament writings. New contexts generated new, more-than-literal interpretations. When John was read in the context of the christological debates that led to the councils of Nicaea (325 A.D.) and Chalcedon (451 A.D.), understandings were generated that were totally unavailable to the evangelist and the communities for whom he originally composed the gospel. Later, John's Gospel was read in the light of the creeds that had become normative for Christian faith. In each instance, reading the text, whether in private or in public, was an event in which the text and the reader or hearers were engaged in a dynamic interaction, one in which the text informed and influenced a process of theological reflection (see Figure 6).

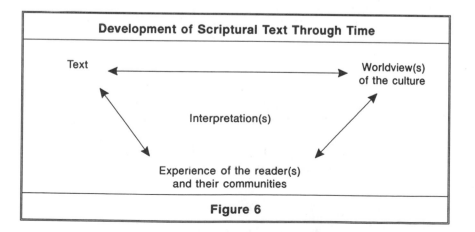

Development of Scriptural Text Through Time

Text ⟷ Worldview(s) of the culture

Interpretation(s)

Experience of the reader(s) and their communities

Figure 6

Reading the Bible in the process of theological reflection today
is also an event of dynamic interaction between the minister and the
text. The quality of that interaction will be determined to a large
extent by the concrete dispositions of the person reading the Bible.
Persons who are unaware of the text's historical setting and world-
view will read it ahistorically, that is, as a text with a life of its own
but unrelated to any particular past experience or situation. Those
who engage the text with awareness of its historical genesis in the
lives of individuals and communities will read it with empathy and
compassion for the human situation in which it came to be Scripture.
These readers will also bring more easily to the text their own experience, both individual and communal. In both cases the dynamic
interaction includes several elements: the text and the reader or
hearer, each with a definite worldview and each in a particular concrete situation (see Figure 7).

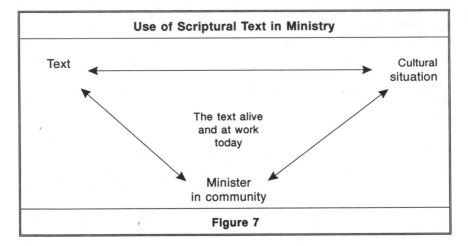

Use of Scriptural Text in Ministry

Text ⟷ Cultural situation

The text alive
and at work
today

Minister
in community

Figure 7

If Scripture provides paradigms for the minister and, more generally, the Christian community, we must still ask: How does the
minister *approach* these texts? What is to be the faith community's
orientation or stance toward Scripture?

This approach is perhaps best described as one of "intimacy"
rather than mastery. For the biblical scholar or church historian the
pressing long-range goal of their study is a mastery of the languages,
cultures, and historical situations which contribute to a reconstruction of what our tradition is and how it was formed. Such mastery is
the lifelong goal of these scholars, a goal rarely attained completely.
Persons in ministry most often have neither the background nor the
time or interest to attempt such mastery. In fact, they do not need to

"master" Scripture. What they do need is enough familiarity to be at ease with the Bible and the skill to bring what they know to bear in the process of theological reflection. This approach of a critical familiarity we may name intimacy.

By intimacy here we do not mean a mystical or nonintellectual approach. Rather, a *more-than*-intellectual grasp of Scripture is envisioned, a grasp which is informed by serious academic study but which "knows from the inside." Faith and understanding are complementary aspects of this relationship. The faith community is invited to this more-than-scientific involvement with these texts as part of the intimacy invitation extended by Jesus Christ to all his followers: "No longer do I call you servants, for the servant does not know what his master is doing; but I have called you friends, for all that I have heard from my Father I have made known to you" (John 15:15). Jesus has called us, he has called us friends, and he has called us to work as his friends. We may never be so comfortable with Scripture that we lose consciousness of this "called" dimension. But we must respond to that call, we must learn to become friends, we must work toward appropriate intimacy with the Word.

The first practical step toward intimacy is getting to know Scripture. The contents of Scripture are, to some degree, already known by the minister and opportunities must be created frequently for rejuvenating and developing that knowledge. But what is important at this stage is getting to know what Scripture is, how it is put together, and thus how to make proper use of its diverse images and stories in pastoral reflections.

This befriending moves between a participation in faith in the biblical writings and an informed, critical understanding of them. Befriending goes beyond a scientific or scholarly grasp of these texts, but also goes beyond an amateur selection of individual passages which seem to fit the mood of an occasion. In seeking to befriend the texts of the Scripture, ministers allow themselves to come under the spell of these texts and experience their own lives being interpreted by them, while simultaneously retaining a critical posture toward the texts as cultural and linguistic products. This, of course, involves considerable tension—as does any act of befriending or intimacy. Ministers cannot avoid this potentially creative tension between participation and criticism, a tension in which the participation of the believer does not obstruct or dissolve criticism and historical and literary criticism does not destroy participation.

To clarify our understanding of the minister's stance toward Scripture, it may be useful to reflect on the different levels of participation involved in the process of befriending classical music. Initially, we participate in the music by listening uncritically to a favorite concerto or symphony. At this point we project onto the music what we want it to mean. But as participation grows, so does our desire to understand the music more critically. So we take time to study the history of music, the development of particular composers, the structure and forms of different types of music, and the themes in this particular composition. We push the music itself away from us and set it at a distance so we can look at it with a more objective and critical eye. In doing so we might suspend for a time our more intimate and total participation, but only so that we might later be able to participate in the music with an appreciation formed and informed by critical understanding.

Participation in the Scriptures, as the first step toward befriending them, can happen in different settings. The minister simply reads the Bible out of interest or for enjoyment. Certain writings are more attractive than others. Some may even be experienced as repugnant. But through reading the Bible and attending to these personal reactions the minister gains an initial familiarity. This familiarity is enhanced when the minister reads the Bible or hears it read in a liturgical context, whether in the Eucharist or in other worship events.

A deeper level of participation is modeled by the use of Scripture in communal prayer. In prayer groups, within the family, and in religious congregations, Christians—convinced that common prayer, rooted in Scripture, is a privileged place to meet the Lord—gather to read and reflect together on the Bible.

The meditative reading of Scripture is still another way to befriend the Bible. This *lectio divina* constitutes a principal activity of traditional monastic life, reinforced in the communal experience of attending to Scripture readings in the daily celebrations of the Divine Office. Methods for the practice of *lectio divina* can be learned easily and many in ministry find this style of prayer helpful. This prayerful exercise demands our full attention and active cooperation, since it approaches Scripture not merely with the intellect but with the full personality.

Ignatian contemplation may also assist the minister in befriending Scripture. In this type of prayer one begins by reading the biblical narrative, then recalling and reconstructing the scene in one's imagination. Involvement grows as the person in prayer gradually enters the biblical scene—seeing the persons, hearing their words, even becoming a participant in the drama. In grace, the person in prayer becomes more deeply aware of the events and how these are a part of her or his own life now. Indeed, Christ himself comes forward to the minister, presenting himself in the mystery being contemplated. What is sought in this contemplation is a deep-felt knowledge of the Lord, a knowledge like that gained through personal contact, shared work, common struggle, and intimate heart-to-heart conversation. Befriending the Scriptures in contemplation means befriending the Lord. Because of the attention needed for this type of prayer, it may be better suited for a time of retreat than for one's regular style of prayer in the midst of a usual daily schedule of activities.

As one participates in the dynamism of the Scriptures in these and other ways, questions will arise that call for a more critical understanding than is available in the prayerful processes of participation. It is the response to these questions that moves the minister into the creative tension between participation and criticism, essential to the process of befriending the Bible as a resource in ministry. Moving from participation to criticism means, as we have said, attending to the text at a distance sufficient to guarantee a more objective and disinterested view. The move is often experienced as involving deprivation and alienation, especially if the prior experiences of prayerful participation have been deeply enriching for the minister. Criticism may seem to threaten the intimacy that has been gained; hence it is resisted. But these feelings can be overcome by the desire to understand the Bible on its own terms and by the conviction that this criticism will, ultimately, enhance one's participation.

These critical questions about a biblical text concern its historical setting and religious milieu, its literary structure and overall movement, the process of its formation, its dominant themes and world-construct, and the detailed exegesis of particular passages. Not all these questions need be addressed at the same time. Nor should the minister expect to have all this information actively available all the time. But once having spent time gaining this information, the minister values it and can retrieve it when desired. We now have widely available the tools through which ministers can gain and refresh this critical understanding of the Bible: *The New Jerome Biblical Commentary, The Anchor Bible Dictionary, Dictionary of Biblical Theology*, and journals such as *The Bible Today*. In education for ministry today (both initial theological study and continuing education), time is well spent in acquainting and reacquainting ministers with the use of these resources.

For the Christian minister this movement between participation and criticism is explicitly informed and influenced by faith. As Christians we believe that the Bible, as the Word of God, is a privileged medium through which God may choose to communicate something to us, as we reach decisions about practical pastoral matters. This faith commitment determines how the minister participates in the text. It also influences how the minister attends to the task of critical understanding. As Krister Stendahl has remarked, contemporary believers have

> the advantage of automatic empathy with the believers in the text—but [their] faith constantly threatens to have [them] modernize the material, if [they do] not exercise the canons of descriptive scholarship rigorously.

While agnostics, Stendahl continues, have

> the advantage of feeling no such temptations, but [their] power of empathy must be considerable if [they are] to identify sufficiently with the believer of the first century. Yet both can work side by side, since no other tools are called for than those of description in the terms indicated by the texts themselves.[12]

What will happen when the minister befriends the Bible through a creative tension between participation and criticism? It is impossible to predict; once the minister enters into this process the outcome simply cannot be controlled. Sometimes, nothing seems to happen. At the end of a busy day I turn to the Bible, with much on my mind, full of concerns and worries. My effort to be attentive expresses my desire to befriend the Bible and my faith that, through it, I remain in contact with God. But distractions abound and I am unmoved.

At other times a deeper degree of participation, now critically informed, may take place. I am pulled into what I read, as my attention, my thoughts, and my feelings become engaged. All else fades to insignificance as I am led to know and love God in and through the text before me. When such a "Word event" may happen is uncontrollable and unpredictable, since it happens by God's activity. We create the climate for it in the ways we befriend the Bible. But it is God who invites us to such a deeper and more meaningful relation.

A critical study of the Scriptures which includes a dissecting of these sacred texts can be an alienating experience for the believer. Paul Ricoeur speaks of the "desert of criticism."[13] Many a minister and ministry student has entered this desert of text and form criticism not to emerge with faith intact. Yet this discipline and desert are necessary for those who would have understanding, as well as faith, inform their pastoral reflections. Beyond this desert lies a "second naïveté" (Ricoeur) toward which we journey all our lives and where participation and criticism mutually illumine our relationship with the Scriptures.

By growing in intimacy with the Scripture through the ongoing dialogue between religious participation and critical understanding, the minister gains the familiarity and skill needed to use the Scriptures well in concrete pastoral situations.

Modes of Attending to Scripture

The conversation with the Bible in this model of theological reflection can begin with a moment of free association in which the minister uses memory and imagination to return to Scripture. This first moment of attending is characterized by an open participation in the texts, as the minister follows whatever associations suggest themselves. For example, a current pastoral concern for the "factions" within the parish can lead to an association with Paul's concern for the "factions" in the church at Corinth (1 Cor. 1:10-17). But the connection may also be experienced at the level of images and symbols, that is, as less rational but every bit as real. The same "factions" might, for example, remind the minister of the struggle between light and darkness in the Gospel of John. Finally, the relationship may be experienced without concepts, images, or symbols but in one's religious consciousness. The minister should be sensitive and open to all three possibilities.

The second moment involves a more disciplined and critical attending to the texts suggested by free association. The minister pushes the text far enough away from the present pastoral concern for it to be examined on its own terms. We offer here one design for how this reflective examination might proceed.

Design for the Critical Examination of a Text in Ministry

Read the passage very carefully, or even *write it out* in sense lines to determine the major divisions of the passage, to get a feel for its overall movement, and to determine the key words and phrases.

- What are the major divisions in the passage?
- What are the key words and phrases?
- What rhetorical or literary techniques are used—questions, antitheses, repetition, etc.?
- What is the overall theme?
- What is the movement of thought?

Situate the passage in its literary, historical, and liturgical contexts. By *literary context*, we mean its place in the particular writing of which it is a part:

- What comes immediately before and immediately after this passage?
- How does this passage fit into the total literary work, the letter, or the gospel?
- What light does its literary context throw on the meaning of the passage?

By *historical context*, we mean the concrete circumstances in which the passage was composed:

- What are the historical circumstances—the time, the place, etc.—in which this writing was composed?
- What were the author and the community for whom this was written experiencing? How did they feel toward each other?

By *liturgical context*, we mean the church's use of this passage in prayer and worship:

- Where does this passage appear in the church's prayer?
- What are the changes, additions, and alterations to the text in the liturgical context?
- What light does the liturgical context throw on the meaning of this passage?

Finally, it is important to *clarify* images, words, or phrases which may remain obscure by consulting one or more commentaries (for example, *The New Jerome Biblical Commentary* or *Harper's Bible Dictionary*), or the notes or annotations in a study Bible.

- What words and phrases need explanation?
- Where do the commentators agree and disagree about the meaning of these images, words, and phrases?
- What opinion do you choose to follow? Why?

Scripture in the Assertion Stage

The role of the Bible at this stage of a pastoral reflection is clarified by recognizing that the sacred texts are themselves a composite of assertions. The plural voices we find in Scripture are not just incidentally different views that have survived due to a lack of edito rial polish. The differences are real; at times they intentionally contrast with each other. Sometimes, the intentional contrast is simply complementary; at other times it is confrontational. The Priestly Writer of the creation story in Genesis, for example, is both intentionally preserving the earlier Yahwist's view on the nature of evil and the relationship between God and humankind (as presented in the story of the Flood) and proposing a complementary view of each. Major differences in theology and in the historical situation in which this later account was formulated led the Priestly Writer to significantly different, but not contradictory, understandings. The author of Job, on the other hand, intentionally and vociferously challenges the theology that characterizes Deuteronomy, Proverbs, the Wisdom psalms, and the prophetic understanding of retribution.

Later, Jesus and the early church, while retaining the Hebrew Scriptures as sacred, nonetheless undertook from the outset a critical interpretation of these texts. While they recognized in the Old Testament the life-creating Word of God, they took the stance that not everything there was of equal importance, not everything was to be understood by Christians in the same way it had been understood in the Jewish community, not everything was to be incorporated by the Christian group as definitive of their relation with God. They exercised a critical discernment in the way they incorporated their tradition. This assertive stance may be recognized in the confrontation of statements attributed in Matthew to Jesus: "You have heard that it was said [followed by a citation of traditional Scripture], but I say to you . . ." (Matt. 5:21, 27, 31, 33, 39, 41).

Thus the Bible is not a book of answers waiting to be matched to contemporary questions, but a set of sometimes complementary, sometimes conflicting, assertions about God among us and about our response to this presence.

A second aid to understanding the role of Scripture in pastoral reflection is to recall how these texts functioned in Christian history. This history is, in fact, the record of Christians' assertive interpretations of the Scriptures in the light of specific cultural and religious concerns. In every age the sacred texts are interpreted in the light of our understanding of our own lives—the meaning of suffering, redemption, justice, freedom, grace. If the New Testament portrays Christ as both suffering and glorified, Christians have at different times in history stressed one of these aspects over the other—not because only one is true and the other false, but because one feature seems so important at the time. Such a stress is an assertion: a definite interpretation of Scripture in the light of a specific, limited concern.

Both the Scriptures as an assertive composition and the assertion of our religious history teach us how we may approach the Bible assertively in our pastoral reflections. Such a practical reflection will always entail a selection, a stressing of *some* passages of Scripture. This is done most critically when we are aware of the historical conditions in which these passages were composed and how they are balanced or even challenged by other texts in Scripture. With such critical awareness we are protected from merely selecting passages which buttress our own unreflective convictions or seem, in a contemporary translation, to give clear answers to complicated problems.

When we assertively and critically set some Scriptural passage in relation to a contemporary cultural or personal experience, we can expect the sacred texts to illumine human action. In this interaction we should also expect these texts themselves to take on new meaning. St. Paul's allusion to the Christian ideal of mutuality in which "there is neither slave nor free, there is neither male nor female" (Gal. 3) means something quite different today than it did two hundred years ago when American Christians held very different opinions about slaves and the role of women in society. The Scriptures are not a "closed book" with a fixed, univocal meaning. On the contrary, as a living revelation, these texts continue to surprise and seize us as we attempt to respond faithfully to ever-different cultural and personal challenges. One way to remain open to this continuing revelation is to continue to assertively grasp and question this source of wisdom.

Scripture and Pastoral Response

The Bible we hold today is the fruit of many critical decisions: the choice, after much debate, to include the Song of Songs despite its highly erotic imagery; the refusal to accept the Gospel of Thomas as an equal of the other gospels; the decision at the beginning of the 16th century to translate the Scripture into the vernacular. Reflective communities today gain confidence by recalling this history—of hesitant decisions and partial insights—a story not unlike that of the contemporary church.[14]

Communities today respond decisively in choosing to make the language of the Bible more inclusive, changing "all men" into "all people," and "brethren" into "sisters and brothers." In this decision a reflective community moves beyond simply receiving the historical text. In this pastoral response, the community participates in the actions by which the church assertively responds to the world. But this stage is possible only if the reflecting minister and community have carefully traversed the earlier stages: critically attending to Scripture and church history and asserting these sources of information against contemporary personal and cultural challenges.[15] Careful attending and assertion will generate insight and suggestions, but the reflective minister and community bring these insights to life in practical decisions. The reflective community *acts*, aware that it responds as part of a larger church, and also aware that its own decisions and actions must remain open to revision and change.

Finally, it is useful to recall that our reading of, listening to and abiding memory of Scripture does, in fact, influence our personal and collective lives. The challenge of a method of reflection is to bring this influence to critical awareness, making it both more conscious and more critical. A developing confidence and competence in the use of Scripture in our lives can make us "critical participants" in these revealing texts. The more thoroughly we befriend this profound source of wisdom, the more powerfully and accurately can it contribute to and shape the reflections and actions which guide our Christian lives.

Notes

1. Since the first edition of this book, theologians have continued to provide excellent resources for ministers who desire to understand better the vital development of the Christian past. For an overview of this history see Jaroslav Pelikan's five volume work *The Christian Tradition* (Chicago, IL: University of Chicago Press, 1971-88). Catherine Mowry LaCugna traces the development of Trinitarian theology in both Eastern and Western Christianity in *God for Us: The Trinity and Christian Life* (HarperSanFrancisco, 1991). In Christology, a wealth of studies have traced the Jewishness of Jesus—a cultural awareness previously forgotten by Christian theologians and ministers; see, for example, Bernard Lee's *The Galilean Jewishness of Jesus* (Mahwah, NJ: Paulist Press, 1991). On the early inchoate development of Christian morality, see Wayne Meeks' *The Origins of Christian Morality: The First Two Centuries* (New Haven: Yale University, 1993). On the historical development of Christian ministry in response to different cultural forces, see Thomas O'Meara's *A Theology of Ministry* (Ramsay, NJ: Paulist Press, 1983). On the changing vision of the Eucharist in Christian tradition, see David Power's *The Eucharistic Mystery: Revitalizing the Tradition* (New York: Crossroad, 1993). Also see Robert Kinast's clear summary of different educational approaches to the tradition in his "Experiencing the Tradition Through Theological Education," in *New Theology Review*, February, 1995.

2. See Richard McBrien's *Catholicism*, new revised edition (HarperSanFrancisco, 1994), p. 62. Research on the Dead Sea Scrolls now helps document this gradual development of the Scriptures; for a discussion see Eugene Ulrich's "The Bible in the Making: The Scriptures at Qumran" in *The Community of the Renewed Covenant: The Notre Dame Symposium on the Dead Sea Scrolls*, ed. E. Ulrich and J. VanderKam (Notre Dame, IN: University of Notre Dame Press, 1994), pp. 77-93.

3. Raymond E. Brown, S.S. and Thomas Aquinas Collins, O.P., "Church Pronouncements," in *The New Jerome Biblical Commentary*, ed. R. E. Brown, J. A. Fitzmyer, and R. E. Murphy (Englewood Cliffs, NJ: Prentice-Hall, 1990), 1173.

4. Raymond Brown finds at least three "different religious groupings" within the developing Johannine community in " 'Other Sheep Not of this Fold': The Johannine Perspective on Christian Diversity in the Late First Century," in *Journal of Biblical Literature 97 (1978):5-22.*

5. For the biblical perspective, see the articles "Exodus," "Redemption," and "Salvation," in X. Léon-Dufour *et al.*, eds, *The Dictionary of Biblical Theology*, trans. P. J. Cahill *et al.*, 2nd ed. rev. (New York: Seabury, 1973).

6. "Israel had been enslaved in Egypt and was to be held there, but its God had wonderfully delivered it from bondage and saved it from the power of the Egyptians. There is no doubt that the concrete statement in this confession is based on a definite historical occurrence and it is not difficult to discern the circumstances in which it took place." Martin Noth, *The History of Israel*, trans. P. Ackroyd, 2nd ed. (London: A. & C. Black 1960), p. 112. See also John Bright, *A History of Israel*, 3rd ed. (Philadelphia: Westminster, 1981), pp. 120-24.

7. The interpretation of a rescue as being due to the favor and causality of one's God was long since established as a traditional religious category in the culture—which extended from Mesopotamia to Egypt—in which Israel was born. "The notion of a God who saves His faithful is common to all religions," "Salvation," in Léon-Dufour, *Dictionary of Biblical Theology*, p. 519. In the "Prayer of Lamentation to Ishtar," the Babylonian goddess receives this request: "I pray to thee, O lady of ladies, goddess of goddesses. O Ishtar . . . , secure my deliverance . . . !" And the Egyptian god, Amon-Re, is addressed: "If I call to thee when I am distressed, thou comest and thou rescuest me . . . Thou art Amon-Re, Lord of Thebes, who rescues . . ." J. Pritchard, ed. *Ancient Near Eastern Texts*, 3rd ed. (Princeton: Princeton University Press, 1969), pp. 384 and 380.

8. The development of the exodus traditions is interwoven with the development of the Pentateuch as a whole. The stages important for our present discussion include: (a) the (probably) oral epic of national religious traditions from the eleventh century, B.C. (i. e., from the period of the Twelve-tribe league after the Exodus [ca. 1280 B.C.] but before the monarchy [ca. 1000 B.C.]); (b) the Yahwist's written account probably from the time of Solomon (900-922 B.C.); (c) The Elohist's written account usually dated to the ninth century B.C.; and (d) the Priestly Writer's reworking of these traditions in the sixth century B.C. See M. Noth, *A History of Pentateuchal Traditions*, trans. B. Anderson (Englewood Cliffs, NJ: Prentice-Hall, 1972), esp. pp. 8-45; and F. M. Cross, *Canaanite Myth and Hebrew Epic* (Cambridge, MA: Harvard University Press, 1973), pp. 293-325. The details above reflect the well-known Documentary Hypothesis. Although there are several contemporary challenges to that hypothesis (e.g. Joseph Blenkin-

sopp's insightful book, *The Pentateuch* [New York: Doubleday, 1992]), the *process* described here remains valid.

9. The Jewish historian, Josephus, in the late first century, A.D., recasts the Exodus narrative in partly similar, partly yet-more-imaginative imagery (Josephus, *Jewish Antiquities* [Loeb, Vol. 4, trans. H. St. J. Thackerary], 2:320-49), though he maintains that "I have recounted each detail here told just as I found it in the sacred books" (2:347).

10. Because the event was so significant for the existence of the people and so characteristic of their saving God, the classic account, already clothed in assorted imaginative details, was subsequently adapted and used (Josh. 3-4) as the libretto for a liturgical celebration (reenacted yearly as the crossing of the Jordan at the shrine of Gilgal) commemorating the event of crossing the Red Sea. That liturgical text, available to the Deuteronomistic Historian in the seventh century B. C., was finally reused as a "historical" episode, forming a link in his history—no longer the link between Egypt and the desert, but typologically transferred to "the people crossing the Jordan into the promised land."

11. "Paradigms are basic models of a vision of life, and of the practice of life, from which flow certain consistent attitudes, outlooks (or "onlooks"), rules and norms of behavior, and specific actions. . . . Rather the paradigm *in* forms and *in*-fluences the life of the community and its members as they become what they are under their own circumstances. By *in*-form I wish to suggest more than giving data or information; I wish to suggest a formation of life. By *in*-fluence I wish to suggest a flowing into the life of the community and its members. A paradigm allows for the community and its members to make it their own, to bring into the texture and fabric of life that exists, conditioned as that is by its historical circumstances, by the sorts of limitations and extensions of particular capacities and powers that exist in persons and communities." See "The Relation of the Gospels to the Moral Life," in D. G. Miller and D. Y. Hadidian, eds., *Jesus and Man's Hope* (Pittsburgh: Pittsburgh Theological Seminary, 1971), 2:111.

12. "Biblical Theology, Contemporary," in *The Interpreter's Dictonary of the Bible* (New York: Abingdon, 1962), 1:422.

13. Paul Ricoeur, *The Symbolism of Evil* (Boston: Beacon Press, 1967), p. 349.

14. See Thomas Kuhn, *The Structure of Scientific Revolutions* (Chicago: University of Chicago Press, 1970), especially the "Postscript" of the 1970 edition, for discussion of the similar inclination of scientists and Christians to explain their respective histories as peaceful and logical developments without disruptions or revolutions. Philosopher Alisdair MacIntyre gives a more realistic portrait of the turbulent history of any tradition: "A living tradition then is a historically extended, socially embodied argument, and an argument precisely in part about the goods which constitute that tradi-

tion." See *After Virtue* (Notre Dame, IN: University of Notre Dame Press, 1981), pp. 206-07.

15. For a reflection on the tension between tradition and contemporary interpretation, see Sandra M. Schneiders, "The Bible and Feminism—Biblical Theology," in *Freeing Theology: The Essentials of Theology in Feminist Perspective*, ed. Catherine Mowry LaCugna (HarperSanFrancisco: 1993), pp. 31-57.

· 3 ·

Experience and Reflection in Ministry

THEOLOGICAL REFLECTION IN MINISTRY IS TRIGGERED BY PARTICULAR PAS-
toral concerns—a community confronting evidence of its own racism;
a question of divorce and remarriage; a parish's responsibility to
those in our neighborhood who are poorly housed. These compelling
concerns arise in personal experience. Brought into the light of the
gospel, our shared experience provokes careful exploration and leads
to generous response.

This model identifies *experience* as a critical voice in the theological conversation. The term itself is notoriously hard to define.
For us, experience refers to all those ideas, feelings, biases and insights that persons and communities bring to the reflection. Experience embraces not only life events, but the conviction and apprehen-
sions and hopes carried in these events.[1]

In this tri-polar model, the experience pole focuses on particular persons and groups. The significant difference between the experience which is *common* within a culture and that which is *particular*
to this minister or this faith community leads us to distinguish
between cultural perspective and personal experience. Personal experience is individual but it is seldom ideosyncratic, since the influence of the surrounding culture is so profound. Still, the experience
of *this* minister and *this* community remain crucial sources in pastoral reflection.[2]

The model acknowledges, too, that experience and tradition
regularly intersect and overlap. Pastoral reflection is an activity of
believing people, people formed within and by a particular religious
heritage. As we gather for pastoral reflection, much of our personal

43

experience has been profoundly shaped by this heritage; it is already Christian. "Already Christian," obviously, does not necessarily mean transformed and sanctified. Our experience may also be shaped by restrictive influences or negative interpretations within the tradition, for example, suspicions surrounding sexuality or the role of women in the church. These instances are not the proudest part of our religious heritage, but they are good examples of how the tradition shapes present personal experience. In reflective faith communities, we come to see how our own experience has been shaped by both religious and cultural influences, often in ways that lead us to gratitude, sometimes in ways that call for conversion.

The Authority of Experience

If experience plays a role in every theological reflection in ministry, the question remains: what is its proper influence? What is its authority?

One response has been that personal experience raises questions that religious tradition then answers. So, becoming aware of our sinfulness we turn to Scripture and the sacraments for healing. Or, feeling sad or disconsolate, we approach the Christian fellowship to find peace and solace. Here the sinfulness and shortcomings of our lives meet God's healing grace, transmitted through our religious tradition. In such a vision of experience, tradition serves as the unique repository of grace. Revelation—the communication of God's love in Jesus Christ—is seen as fully given and available to us in a "deposit of faith" guarded and administered by church leaders. Personal experience plays little active role in this drama and enjoys no special authority in Christian reflection. Experience is essentially grist for the purifying mill of ecclesial instruction.

Another vision of God's self-revelation suggests a more dynamic role for experience. We remember that Scripture itself is the record of a people's experience of God's presence among them. We recall that when our life experience and our religious heritage enter into dialogue, a vital and volatile conversation ensues. In this conversation our experience, attentively discerned and courageously purified, serves to both confirm and question the adequacy of our common heritage.

Turning to Scripture, we find again and again stories of faith as a journey. God has led our ancestors along strange paths and through circuitous routes toward grace and healing. These journeys have included long seasons in the desert; detours, dead-ends and bad judgments were part of these adventures. Jesus' own journey through death to new life included failure and public humiliation.

Given the chance to reflect, we notice how our own lives echo and affirm these Scriptural accounts. We too are familiar with wrong turns, blind alleys, missteps along the way. Attesting to this resonance between tradition and experience, our lives become further testimony, reinforcing the scriptural account of faith.

Revelation—God's self-disclosure which surprises us, overturns our certitudes and transcends our best imaginings—is *registered* in experience.[3] Bringing God's revelation into experience's intimate embrace does not diminish Scripture's holiness or compromise God's transcendence; rather it opens us more fully to the meaning of Incarnation. The religious authority of experience is rooted in a recognition of God's continuing, disturbing presence among us. When our experience (of sin and forgiveness; of dying and rising; of Christ recognized in the stranger) confirms the testimony of Scripture and the wisdom of our religious heritage, it *authorizes* the Christian tradition again. By saying "yes!" to this sacred story, affirmed again in our own experience, the faith community regenerates the Christian heritage in its own time.

This incarnational optimism allows Christians to listen confidently to the three different sources of this model; it is the same God who acts mysteriously in all three contexts. The voice of the tradition enjoys a special authority in our lives, but its privileged position does not replace or substitute for the authority of our own life experiences. These experiences, too, have their own religious integrity. Human experience is not transformed by a simple exposure to revelation transmitted within a religious body; our lives are transformed by *engaging* this tradition. Itself open to the gracious advent of God, personal experience—along with the religious tradition—serves as a genuine source for theological reflection.

As a component in theological reflection, experience overlaps with tradition in another important way. The lives of adult Christians, with their decades of experience in living the Christian life, are a small but significant part of the larger Christian tradition. As believers, our lives represent ways in which the Christian vision may be lived. Alternating between sin and faithfulness, between seasons of authentic faith and periods of confusion, our lives are not unlike the larger tradition itself. Although they represent only a partial perspective on Christian life, gatherings of the faithful today are themselves integral to the Christian tradition. It is in the current experience of faith communities that the Christian tradition enters the present and is transmitted to the future.

Befriending Experience

Experience can serve as a genuine conversation partner in theological reflection in ministry only if we learn how to listen to it and purify it. An appeal to experience does not mean abandonment to whatever crosses our mind or stirs our fancy. The commitment to experience's theological value does not endorse a collapse into relativism: "everyone is entitled to his or her own opinion."

The experience of an individual Christian and a particular faith community becomes a reliable member of the conversation only when we attend to it with great care. The discipline of communal reflection requires that we *submit our experience to patient scrutiny in the company of seasoned Christians*. At one extreme we may be swept away by our experience: "I am right and anyone who objects is simply wrong!" (With such conviction, there is no need for a conversation.) But, in our pastoral experience, the more frequent temptation for many people is to ignore or deny their experience. The reflective method leads us between these extremes. Its discipline begins in believing that our experience is worth listening to; the discipline continues in willingness to learn ways to bring our experience into the communal setting.

When we attend to experience, *what* are we listening to and *how* do we pay attention? If experience refers simply to what we *consciously think* about a pastoral concern, we can just take note of these ideas and move on to the next step of the reflection. In this method, however, *experience* includes feelings as well as explicit ideas, along with those biases and convictions of which we are only vaguely aware.

This method of pastoral reflection attempts to gain access to different levels of our experience. Since these levels go well beyond the rational (what we can immediately recall as we think about this question), we need *extra-rational* means of access as well. Extra-rational refers to the various emotional overtones and imaginative states that, along with our conscious thoughts, constitute the wide range of human awareness. The word *extra-rational* suggests that emotions and imagination are ways of knowing that complement our analytic abilities. The word *extra-rational* also points, in ways that the terms *irrational* and *nonrational* do not, to the positive contribution of images and feelings to pastoral reflection.

Two examples from our own work may illustrate how reflective groups gain access to these extra-rational resources. As Christians we confess we are *children of God*, not only at birth or baptism but throughout our life. But what practical relevance does this traditional conviction have? How do people experience themselves as children of God? In discussing the shape of contemporary Christian spirituality, we have invited groups to reflect on childhood as a season for learning how to trust and how to play. In a prayerful moment, people revisit in memory a time in childhood when they were held or cared for in a special way. Next they recall an experience of play, whether with a childhood friend or by themselves. Finally they are asked how *child of God* describes them today. A question helps the reflection be more concrete: "what strategy do you use to keep the child of God alive in your life?" An exercise like this gives participants the opportunity to move this central Christian image beyond rhetoric into their experience. A person caught up in many adult responsibilities may find that the child is almost entirely absent from her life; this realization provokes her to make some changes. Another person is surprised how aptly *child of God* describes his self-awareness; this insight moves him to a prayer of gratitude, reinforcing the determination to keep this sense of the child vital in his life.

Guided fantasy provides another avenue of access to imagination. Approaching a critical pastoral question, a faith community needs to become aware of its feelings about the Christian tradition and the authority and weight of its religious past. So in preparing groups to use the tri-polar method, we often begin with a guided fantasy on Christian tradition itself. The goal at this point is not clarifying theological content but exploring people's attitudes—attitudes that will influence how they approach the tradition as a resource in pastoral reflection. After an exercise to bring the group into a prayerful and centered mood, we ask participants to visualize the word *tradition* and then to hold themselves attentive to the range of images that arise. Responses vary, with many surprises. One person confronts an immovable fortress, threatening and ominous. Another sees an ocean liner moving carefully but persistently through a turbulent sea. Someone encounters a compassionate sage, withered and wise; someone else wanders in a graveyard. Yet another climbs among the limbs of a giant tree—alive, strong, protective.

A common error early in group reflection is to assume that we all mean the same thing when we use a common word—like *tradition*. An exercise like this helps people appreciate the multiple meanings and myriad feelings that surround the term. At this initial stage the question is not which of these images is "right." Rather, the goal is attending to the group's experience at the extra-rational level—both to clarify the different starting points among us and to become more explicitly aware of the emotions we bring to the reflection.

Few adults are fully aware of the range of their emotional responses; fewer still are comfortable with these feelings. As Christians, many of us have learned that feelings reflect our most selfish needs. Emotions are judged to be volatile, unreliable, "merely" subjective. Traditionally, the attention given to feelings was preeminently for control rather than for critical clarification. Feelings were evaluated rather than explored, short-circuiting any attempt to find fresh meaning here. Lacking both tools and encouragement to listen carefully to emotions and imagination, many groups—not surprisingly—attempt to outlaw feelings from their formal interaction. This strategy seldom works. Worse, it blocks the group's ability to bring imagination and emotion as resources to pastoral decision making. The tri-polar method calls for critical access to both feelings and imagination, so that these revealing aspects of experience may contribute explicitly to theological reflection.[4]

Missing Voices

When a reflecting community learns to value experience, it begins to notice the absence of certain voices in the on-going conversation of faith. The experience that has guided theological reflection over many centuries has been men's. The work of feminist theologians shows how a dominant culture of patriarchy has distorted the acoustics of the community of faith, muting women's voices and impoverishing the tradition.[5] Women who find that this distortion has been fatal have little choice but to leave their religious heritage. But many women judge that the injury is grave but not mortal; by reclaiming the experience of women and other historically-silenced groups, we give voice to the full redemptive witness of Jesus Christ.

Spirituality offers an example of how women's experience is changing theological discourse. For centuries, a spirituality of detachment prevailed in Christian piety: through self-control, a holy Christian must detach himself from the temptations of the world. Just as a man-child must move away from his mother to find his own identity and independence, so the Christian must separate himself from compromising allegiances and dependencies.

This "masculine" ideal of detachment led theologians like Ambrose to define the virtue of integrity in an individualist fashion. As historian Peter Brown illustrates, Ambrose pictured integrity as the sharp-edged definition of self, distinct and separate from the influence of others.[6] A person's integrity was centered in his singularity and was compromised by contact with others—a contact that Ambrose described as "feminizing." The ideal of integrity for Ambrose was the virgin, untouched and uncompromised by others' influence.

Such a spirituality of detachment casts a long shadow over all relationships. In this spiritual climate, every bond risks becoming a clinging dependency. Today feminist theologians show us how a spirituality of detachment distorts the experience of both women and men. Attachment describes our commitments—to persons, to values, to faith. Fidelity itself is a form of attachment; it is through the virtues of hope and faith that we cling to God. Followers of Christ must learn to be *both* detached and engaged. A discipline of detachment, fuelled by a man's concern for independence and self-control, can end in the neglect of the disciplines of engagement.

Balancing detachment (and the masculine fascination for control) with a spirituality of engagement, we reclaim a richer vision of integrity. Because we are the body of Christ, our integrity can never be simply individual. Christian integrity is based on the communion of many in the one assembly. The ideal of remaining individually "intact," untouched by others' influence, is an illusion. We begin our lives in the womb, securely anchored to another person. As adults our best efforts of love and work are rooted in fruitful attachments to one another and to God. Other people are not simply threats to our separate integrity; they are the partners with whom we find our integrity as the body of Christ. Listening to women's voices, the church rediscovers a vision of engagement and integrity that it was in danger of losing.

Other powerful voices, long muted in our religious tradition, are being raised up to enrich the conversation about Christian faith. In this country, for example, communities with diverse cultural roots—African-American, Hispanic, Eastern European, Native American, Vietnamese—are entering the dialogue, eager to share their perspectives on justice, worship, family and leadership. The influence of these rich experiences of faith promises to re-define Christianity in the United States in the 21st century.[7]

Privileged Experience

Theological reflection that systematically excludes or ignores part of the body of Christ distorts the experience of faith. But in a conversation of many voices, whose experience claims our common attention? Here again Scripture is our guide. The Bible turns again and again to the oppressed in their struggle for justice. This tradition begins among the Hebrews enslaved in Egypt; it continues in the prophets' concern for the *anawim*—the poor and dispossessed in whom Yahweh takes special interest. Jesus reaffirmed this tradition in his sermon on the mount: "Blessed are the poor, for theirs is the kingdom of heaven (Luke 6:20). . . . Blessed are those who hunger and thirst for justice, for they will be filled" (Matthew 5:6).

What is the revelation here? Is this more than a romanticizing of poverty? What is the special merit of suffering and the longing for justice? Why are such experiences—in the Scriptures and in our lives—so privileged? Perhaps this priority is to counterbalance the human impulse to separate ourselves from other people's suffering and to insulate "our kind" from responsibility in their plight. Satisfying this impulse, we soon find ourselves imbedded in self-righteousness or mired in boredom. We are safe but, with little thirst for justice, distant from God.

But experience, come as chance or grace, puts our safe distance in doubt. Perhaps we visit a soup kitchen or an AIDS hospice. Or we share the Eucharist with someone who is homeless or a dispossessed family in flight from political terror. In this gathering of the marginalized—"the lowly" of the Hebrew Scriptures and Mary's Magnificat—we hear again the sound of our redemption breaking through our righteousness and boredom. Suddenly the Eucharist comes alive; we are in the presence of Jesus under the shadow of his cross.

Or the revelation arrives as a serious illness or family crisis that ushers us into the house of "the lowly." Striken by some loss, we watch our confidence and our plans fall away. The distress wrenches us open to beliefs we had all but abandoned. Self-sufficiency and self-righteousness are burned away; in their ashes faith stirs again.

Theologian James Poling suggests that theological reflection "begins with the presence of difference and otherness in experience."[8] As long as our personal experience and our religious heritage seem to fit comfortably ("God's in his heaven; all's right with the world"), there is no special need for reflection and the purification it brings. Otherness—in the face of the poor and the sick and the outcast—interjects tension into our shared life of faith. In these disruptive experiences life becomes more urgent, more charged with meaning. Our discomfort sets us on the journey toward conversion. Religious hope rekindles as we sense the call to live more faithfully, more courageously.

The Sense of the Faithful

The conversation between experience and the Christian tradition brings us back to the elusive image of *sensus fidelium*. A gathering of mature Christians bears within itself a "sense" or instinct for recognizing God's presence in their lives. How does a method of pastoral reflection assist a group to recognize and trust its own sense of faith? How can community leaders help this instinct mature?

Sometimes the sense of the faithful is described as a universal agreement throughout the church. But in this season of change we can expect more diversity. The sense of the faithful is not an automatic acquiescence in which each parish and diocese consents to what it has received. The *sensus fidelium* is an active conviction through which a faith community witnesses to the larger church.

The sense of the faithful alerts us to the expectable vitality of a believing community, its own particular awareness of Christian life and of how this witness is to be expressed in the world. This notion is admittedly dangerous; it can be used to justify a group's wrong-headed pursuit of narrow self-interest to the neglect of the wider church. We must resist the temptation to reduce this mysterious dynamic in the body of Christ to opinion poles or vote counts. Yet reaffirming the importance of the *sensus fidelium* is essential today. Recognizing this communal instinct, we acknowledge the need for faith communities to be critically in touch with their religious hopes and particular vocation. The underlying conviction is that this sense of the faithful, carefully examined and purified, will contribute to the larger church through both support and challenge. The path to a revitalized *sensus fidelium* lies in the development of methods by which a community can become more critically conscious of its own experience: how this experience has already been "Christianized" and how its limited insights can be part of the on-going purification of the tradition itself.

In pastoral reflection we perform those functions that comprise the *sensus fidelium*, as we "cling without fail to the faith once delivered to the Saints, penetrate it more deeply by accurate insights, and apply it more thoroughly to life."[9] An ongoing reflection on our experience of faith can strengthen this communal instinct. When that happens, this model of theological reflection has reached its goal.

Notes

1. On the new enthusiasm for the role of experience in theological reflection see Donald Gelpi's *The Turn to Experience in Contemporary Theology* (Mahwah, NJ: Paulist Press, 1994), and George Schner's "The Appeal to Experience," in *Theological Studies* 53 (1992), pp. 40-59. For reflections on the role of experience in pastoral reflection, see Patricia O'Connell Killen and John de Beer's *The Art of Theological Reflection* (New York: Crossroad, 1994), pp. 21ff; and Robert Kinast's "Experiencing the Tradition through Theological Reflection," *New Theology Review* (February 1995).

2. Avery Dulles, in an otherwise favorable review of Tracy's *Blessed Rage for Order*, has objected to Tracy's restriction of *experience* to common human

experience. Dulles suggests a third source for theological reflection: "Christian experience, i.e., the kind of ecstatic or peak experience to which the New Testament, for example, bears witness." (See *Theological Studies*, 37 [June, 1976], p. 308.) In a footnote here, Dulles writes: "By 'Christian experience,' I mean experience that is intrinsically qualified by the Christian symbols through which it is communicated and expressed." Dulles' concern for a specifically Christian experience is more likely to be honored if a method of reflection distinguishes between broad cultural experience and the experience of this believing community.

3. See Mary Catherine Hickert's "Experience and Tradition—Can the Center Hold?" in *Freeing Theology*, Catherine Mowry LaCugna, ed. (HarperSanFrancisco, 1993). Though revelation transcends human experience, it "can be perceived and responded to only in and through human categories" (p. 63). Also see Thomas O'Meara's "Toward a Subjective Theology of Revelation," in *Theological Studies*, 36 (September, 1975), p. 410-27, and David Tracy's "The Particularity and Universality of Christian Revelation," in *Revelation and Experience*, Edward Schillebeeckx and Bas Van Iersel, eds. (New York: Seabury, 1979), especially 109-15.

4. In *The Inner Rainbow: The Imagination in Christian Life* (New York: Paulist Press, 1983), Kathleen Fischer offers a practical guide to the use of imagination in pastoral reflection and in other aspects of Christian living.

5. For excellent analyses of the new attention to women's experience, see Elizabeth Johnson's *She Who Is: The Mystery of God in Feminist Theological Discourse* (New York: Crossroad, 1994); Anne Carr's *Transforming Grace: Christian Tradition and Women's Experience* (New York; Harper & Row, 1990); and Letty Russell, Pui-lan Kwok, Ada María Isasi-Díaz, and Kate Geneva Cannon, *Inheriting Our Mother's Gardens: Feminist Theology in Third World Perspective* (Philadelphia, PA: Westminster, 1988). For a cautionary note on experience, see Sheila Greeve Davaney's "The Limits to the Appeal to Women's Experience," in *Shaping New Vision: Gender and Values in American Culture*, Clarissa W. Atkinson, Constance H. Buchanan, and Margaret Miles, eds. (Ann Arbor, MI: UMI Research Press, 1987), pp. 31-49.

6. See Peter Brown's magisterial study *The Body and Society* (New York: Columbia University Press, 1988); pages 341-55. Brown sums up Ambrose's vision of Christian identity: "To surrender any boundary line was to court the ancient shame of the Roman male—it was to "become soft," to be "effeminated" (p. 347). Brown describes Ambrose's vision of *integritas* as "the precious ability to keep what was one's own untarnished by alien intrusion" (p. 354).

7. In *Black Theology: A Documentary History*, Vol. I & II (Maryknoll, NY: Orbis, 1994), James H. Cone and Gayard S. Wilmore gather classic sources to trace the emergence of African-American theology in the U.S.; see also the February 1994 issue of the *New Theology Review* for a series of articles on African-American experiences in American Catholicism. And in *The Galilean Journey* (Maryknoll, NY: Orbis, 1983), Virgilio Elizondo energizes theo-

logical reflection by celebrating the place of *mestizaje* (mixed-blood heritage) and *fiesta* in Hispanic spirituality. See also Ada María Isasi-Díaz and Yolanda Tarango, *Hispanic Women: Prophetic Voice in the Church* (Minneapolis: Fortress Press, 1992).

8. For Poling, pastoral reflection is "theological interpretation of unheard voices of personal and community life for the purpose of continual transformation of faith in the true God of love and power toward renewed ministry practice;" *The Abuse of Power* (Nashville, TN: Abingdon Press, 1991), p. 187. See also Paulo Freire, *The Pedagogy of the Oppressed* (New York: Continuum, 1983) and Susan Brooks Thistlethwaite and Mary Potter Engel, eds., *Constructing Christian Theologies from the Underside* (New York: Harper and Row, 1990).

9. This description of *sensus fidelium* appears in The Dogmatic Constitution on the Church (*Lumen Gentium*), Paragraph Twelve; see *The Documents of Vatican II*, edited by Walter M. Abbott, (New York: America Press, 1966), pp. 29-30.

· 4 ·

The Conversation with Culture

TO READ THE SIGNS OF THE TIMES, TO HEAR THE VOICES OF THE age—these evocative images challenge the community of faith to strengthen its dialogue with the culture in which it lives. The model we explore in this book incorporates this challenge by identifying culture as an indispensable component in theological reflection in ministry.

The relationship of a culture—its convictions, biases, insights—to a religious tradition and so to theological reflection has an ambiguous and intriguing history. Through the first half of this century, for example, academic theology found its chief conversation partner in philosophy. And in the pastoral life of the churches, religious reflection often took the form of applying to one's life "in the world" the moral conclusions that were reached in the explicitly religious settings of biblical study or a devotional life of prayer. Today the world-view of believers is increasingly shaped by the categories of the social sciences, especially psychology, sociology, economics. And no longer content with an antagonistic juxtaposition of *church* and *world*, most people of faith recognize a richer interaction between faith and culture. The tri-polar method addresses this reciprocal interaction. By giving explicit attention to the *cultural pole*, the method both helps communities identify the multiple influences already at play and encourages communities to explore cultural resources that can enrich their life of faith.

Distinguishing culture as a separate element in the model carries both benefits and risks. The chief benefit is clarity. A model attempts to simplify a complex process so that it can be better understood. In this way, separating out three poles of pastoral reflection is something like stopping a propeller to examine its component parts. When an aircraft is in flight, the blades of the propeller are invisible to the human eye. If we want to see clearly the components (in our airplane example, the blades) we have to stop the process (the flight). To be sure, this static view gives us only a partial understanding of how an aircraft flies. But looking closely at the components can expand our awareness of the critical elements in the process. So the tri-polar model attempts to clarify the process of pastoral reflection by looking closely at three essential components.

But distinguishing these three components runs the risk of implying that each pole of the model is actually discrete and disconnected from the others. The truth of the matter is otherwise; *theological reflection* names an ongoing process of both mutual construction and mutual critique. We must take care that the model's pursuit of clarity does not mask this deeper dynamic in effective pastoral reflection. While highlighting these three potential sources of religious insight (tradition, experience, culture), the method continues to emphasize the overlap and interplay among them.

In our initial discussion of the tri-polar model in Chapter One we noted that the cultural pole represents not a realm of unredeemed nature, but a mixed environment, partly antithetical and partly complementary to Christian vision. The reflective community cannot ignore its cultural context, or, perhaps more exactly, the community ignores these influential factors only to its detriment. Pastoral theologian Michael Cowan notes, "The Christian community of faith will sometimes affirm the workings of its surrounding culture and society; sometimes it will confront them. It is never unaffected by them; it never fails to affect them. Those, including ministers and ministerial leaders, who do not understand the cultural worlds in which they act, act blindly and, even worse, disrespectfully."[1]

Only by dealing with culture as an explicit component of pastoral reflection is the faith community in a position to recognize and overcome negative cultural influences and to harness and use its complementary forces. Such a community attunes itself to the call to judgment that sometimes sounds in a culture's voice, challenging church structures that have drifted away from the gospel norm and religious practices that have lost authenticity.

Contributions of the Cultural Pole

The cultural pole of the model strengthens pastoral reflection in three ways. Recognizing this essential component (1) alerts us to culture's role in shaping human experience, (2) acknowledges the mutual critique of tradition and culture, and (3) encourages the community of faith to actively engage cultural information and resources in its mission and ministry.

1. Culture's Role in Shaping Human Experience

Since the 1960s, the understanding of culture has been increasingly influenced by the semiotic perspective.[2] Semiotics stresses how culture shapes experience. Reality does not exist as "raw data" that all human beings interpret the same way. Instead, human experience always comes "cooked"—seasoned in the communal pot, part of a cultural stew of expectations and prohibitions, of significance and symbol, that prevail in any group. We know the world only in culturally-formed ways.

In his influential book *The Interpretation of Cultures*, Clifford Geertz defines culture as "an historically transmitted pattern of meanings embodied in symbols . . . by means of which persons communicate, perpetuate and develop their knowledge about and attitudes toward life."[3] Theologian Don Browning highlights components of culture which most directly influence theology and ministry. For Browning, culture means "a set of symbols, stories (myths), and norms for conduct that orient a society or group cognitively, affectively, and behaviorally to the world in which it lives."[4]

In these definitions, *culture* designates the assumptive world of a group of people. Culture in this sense is largely invisible to us, functioning primarily through common sense understandings of reality ("This is how the world is") and widely accepted expectations of appropriate behavior ("This is how we do it around here"). In this meaning, culture serves not as *one* of the poles of pastoral reflection but as a formative ambience that shapes all three poles.

Since culture in this sense functions mostly outside explicit awareness, one goal of pastoral reflection is to help us become more aware of the cultural forces at play. Gaining perspective on our assumptive world is not easy, because these assumptions are the lenses through which we view life. Reflection asks us to *look at* rather than *look through* these lenses. Such critical examination can be disconcerting, leaving us with a sense that our world is out of focus.

Examining our culture's assumptions calls into question the world-view that makes sense to us, the perspective through which we make sense of our own lives. Religious assumptions, too, come under review as we recognize ways that cultural attitudes and social arrangements influence the faith tradition itself. These cultural dynamics have shaped not only traditonal formulations of religious doctrines and conventional structures of denominational life but also the consciousness of believers. Both subtly and significantly, cultural assumptions and religious convictions are intertwined. As believing people recognize these connections, their grasp of the faith tradition expands into an embrace that is both appreciative and critical.

Reflective believers today better understand that the Christianity we have received is not "culture free" but comes wrapped in habits of different social settings and earlier times. Reflecting on culture's formative role in its own religious heritage deepens a group's spiritual maturity, but this maturity seldom comes without distress. Faithful people find themselves questioning convictions and practices previously taken-for-granted. Communities experience a wide range of responses—agreement, disagreement, surprise, confusion, conflict, resistance—all carrying strong emotion. Both groups and individuals are tempted to turn away from the reflection that triggers such strong feelings. At this point, having a shared method strengthens a faith community's resolve by showing members how to proceed. Method holds the group in faith, signaling that their confusion is expectable and predicting that grace will sustain them in their communal search.

2. Culture and Tradition in Mutual Critique

In this model of reflection, religion and culture cannot be simplisticly dichotomized. God does not abide unambiguously in the Christian tradition nor Mammon in the culture. God's presence in the world is not restricted within the confines of denominational life; God's action can be discerned in cultural life as well as in an explicitly religious heritage.[5] Thus culture remains an ambiguous environment, incorporating values and structures inimical to the best insights of the religious tradition as well as insights and resources that support the tradition's continuing purification and growth.

The conversation between culture and religious tradition can move in three directions: (a) the religious tradition challenges the culture; (b) the religious tradition is challenged by the culture; (c) the religious tradition engages the resources of the culture in pursuit of its own religious mission.[6]

The first stance shows Christianity's prophetic role: the gospel vision calls to account those institutions and values which, oppressive and false, deny the life of the Spirit. Here the religious tradition supports the faith community's challenge to the *status quo*, even at the risk of culture's retribution. The courageous witness of Archbishop Oscar Romero in El Salvador reminds us of the price Christianity's prophetic stance may exact.

The second stance acknowledges developments within the culture that call the religious community to self-examination. Thus the civil rights movement in the United States has confronted Christians with facts of personal and institutional racism within the church. The women's movement, now of international scope, challenges religious institutions to examine their language and structures for evidence of implicit and explicit sexism. Movements for liberation in the Third World force the churches to examine their support of, and even identification with, colonialism and capitalism. These cultural movements, themselves often deeply influenced by religious convictions, challenge Christianity to self-examination and purification.

In the third stance the religious tradition uses the resources of the culture in pursuit of its own religious mission. These resources range from philosophy, political interpretation and the social sciences to other religious traditions such as Islam or Buddhism. In the following section we will focus on the social sciences, exploring potential contributions to the faith community's ministry.

3. Culture Resources for Mission and Ministry

Pastoral reflection begins, as theologian Jack Shea notes, in the questions that people ask about "what is creative and destructive in their interpersonal lives and the systems in which they live."[7] The social sciences provide tools for understanding these forces. Taken alone, strategies and solutions generated in the social sciences fall short of a genuinely religious reflection. But the social sciences contribute to the pastoral conversation a critical perspective and a fund of information, both indispensable in contemporary ministry. In the next section, we will explore three ways in which the social sciences may contribute to theological reflection in ministry.

Social Sciences and the Intellectual Perspective of the Age

In every era of Christian history, theology has found itself in dialogue with the dominant intellectual categories of the time. In this long dialogue, Greek philosophers, especially Plato and Aristotle, have spoken persuasively. In this century the development of the social sciences has provided a new and significant conversation partner for theological reflection. Theologian Karl Rahner, especially in his later work, noted this shift: "theology may find its most significant dialogical partner not in philosophy but in the natural, psychological, and social sciences which shape [human] self-understanding in the present."[8] Don Browning stresses the contemporary function of the social sciences as "coordinating models," analogous to the pervading myths and theological images that supported a sense of shared meaning in previous cultures. These models shape the basic intellectual and emotional categories of contemporary life: "They give certain members of the society (for instance, its intellectual elites) kinds of maps which orient them to their worlds, tell them what to trust, what to hope for, and how to get what they have come to believe is good."[9]

In our own work we draw on two areas of social science theory and research that touch on issues especially relevant in ministry today: the nature and possibility of the human person and the structure and dynamic of human community. Religious questions about vocation, personal morality, and spirituality will be necessarily related to the surrounding culture's philosophical and psychological interpretations of human life and development.

More specifically, the growth of developmental psychology over the past several decades has made available to theological reflection a clearer awareness of the differing challenges encountered over the lengthening life span of adults today. This delineation of specific challenges in the psychosocial maturing process represents a significant contribution to a contemporary Christian spirituality of adult maturity and holiness.[10] Here, the role of such cultural information becomes clear: it can neither be allowed to *determine* the shape of Christian spirituality (this happens, for instance, when cultural ideals overwhelm theological conviction, producing a short-lived fad), nor can such information be ignored in the pursuit of a "pure" and unchanging understanding of religious growth.

Another significant contribution to theological reflection in ministry may be drawn from sociology's inquiry into community. Pastoral reflection is almost always concerned with the style of our life together—its potential and its challenges. Sociological theory and research concerning contemporary forms of community can contribute to theological reflection by pointing to specific problems of community life today and by suggesting strategies of clarification and conflict resolution which facilitate the formation and growth of community.[11] Here again, this sociological information is neither simply to replace inherited models and convictions about Christian community nor is it to be ignored in an effort to safeguard the uniqueness of the church.

Social Sciences and the Self-Purification of the Church

Social actions have social consequences, some of which are unexpected. This basic sociological insight helps the church remain faithful to its religious mission in the midst of changing historical and social circumstances.

To understand an institution like religion, we have to look not only at its *intentions* (the values and ideals the church professes) but also at its *effects* (how people and society are affected by what the church does). Examining these social consequences closely, we sometimes see that the effects of the church's public action turn out to be at odds with the church's best hopes. The lesson here is that to judge religion in terms of its explicit values alone is to understand it not *incorrectly* but *partially*.

In *Religion and Alienation*, theologian Gregory Baum explores sociology's potential contribution to a faith community that knows itself to be always in need of reform. "Religion," Baum notes, "has a social impact which may be hidden from the theologian."[12] For example, the establishment in the sixteenth century of seminaries to upgrade the quality of professional ministry in the church (religiously positive motive) reinforced the gap between clergy and laity (religiously negative effect). On the contemporary scene, the church's stress on the importance of marriage and family life (religiously positive intention) may result in the neglect of an effective ministry to unmarried, widowed, separated or divorced persons (religiously negative effect). Examining the consequences of its public actions, the faith community will discern what are the unintended, unanticipated, and even undesirable effects.

Baum challenges religious leaders, and the faith community more broadly, to acknowledge these unintended, unanticipated, even undesirable effects of its public life. This self-corrective function of the religious tradition he calls critical theology. The word *critical* does not designate a separate area of theological study; rather it describes a sensitivity that should characterize any theological reflection. This critical stance alerts us to the social consequences of theological belief and religious practice, reminding us that religiously correct motivation can nevertheless lead to actions that have religiously negative effect. Leaders in the religious community are at least naive and probably even negligent if they do not incorporate this insight in understanding and evaluating their own activities.[13]

Mature sociological awareness, having itself moved beyond the temptations of reductionism, can assist the faith community to be accountable for the structural consequences of religious belief and behavior. But ultimately it is the gospel which provides the criteria the community will use to form and reform the church's institutional life.

Social Sciences Provide Tools for Ministry

Thus far we have discussed primarily the ways in which the *theoretical perspective* and *analytic categories* of the social sciences may serve as resources to the religious tradition. The *methods* and *findings* of the social sciences are valuable as well. Van Campenhoudt discusses this role of the social sciences:

> "When a pastoral decision has to be made, the appeal to theology is not enough, for today, more than ever, all decision making requires a precise, scientific knowledge of reality, and it is not the role of theology, but rather that of the social sciences, to provide us with such information."[14]

The community of faith may take advantage of the methods or findings of the social sciences to better carry out its ministry in a variety of ways. First, the empirical methods of data gathering and analysis can be used to provide accurate information about issues facing the religious community. Thus, statistics concerning population changes, or information about the incidence of unemployment, or an assessment of the needs experienced by recently divorced parents can contribute significantly to the shape of an effective ministry."[15]

Second, the religious tradition can define a problem according to its own criteria and then use social science research methods to test a hypothesis or to achieve a more accurate description of the problem. For example, many denominations have used sociological and psychological analysis to help them develop new criteria for recruiting, evaluating and training candidates to assume positions of leadership in vastly changing ministry settings.

Third, the religious tradition can adopt the techniques and tools developed in the social sciences for use in pursuit of its own goals. Thus, religious persons have become trained in and use therapeutic techniques developed in the psychological disciplines, skills of management and planning developed in organizational development, and skills of small group interaction and problem solving developed in the communication disciplines. The Alban Institute in Washington, D.C., for example, has made these resources available to local congregations and ministers from a range of Christian denominations for over twenty-five years.

Finally, the social sciences can provide information and interpretation on questions that are of independent interest to the religious community. It can be useful for the minister to see how a particular question is understood and evaluated by the social scientist, not necessarily in order that the minister will see it that way, but because seeing a complex problem from another point of view can often enhance one's understanding. Thus, the minister will have an even better appreciation of the question when it is understood in the Christian perspective.

Conclusion

The Christian conversation between faith and culture begins in the prologue of St. John's Gospel: "He was in the world, and the world came into being through him; yet the world did not know him." (1:10) Throughout, this gospel describes a powerful antagonism between God's presence and "the world (which) cannot receive (the Spirit) because it neither sees him nor knows him." (14:17) Yet in the midst of this discouraging dialogue we hear a startling reversal: "God so loved the world that God sent God's only son . . . " (3:16) Recognizing the world thus, as an enduring object of God's affection, gives the conversation a more optimistic tone.

For two thousand years the followers of Jesus have continued this debate concerning the peril and hope of living in the world. Two powerful temptations repeatedly sweep through Christian life. The first is the desire to abandon the world and find a more perfect life elsewhere, perhaps in the desert, perhaps after death. The second is the illusory ambition to bring culture into such comformity with the gospel that a Christian state will be produced. Both longings defeat the tension that seems an indispensable aspect of following Christ in our time.

Theologian Avery Dulles describes three attitudes toward culture he sees at play within the Catholic community in the United States.[16] The first is a nostalgia for the European cultural trappings of pre-Vatican II Catholicism; the second risks an indiscriminate pluralism by losing sight of the genuine limits of America's cultural perspective. Dulles' third alternative, similar to the approach of this method, attempts to establish a crital dialogue with the dominant culture. Respectful of our culture's defining values, the faith community stands ready to contribute actively to the common good. But we must nevertheless stand ready to challenge the culture on critical aspects of civic life, whether capital punishment or immigration policy or military intervention.

Similarly, theologian Don Browning calls for a dialogue of mutual exploration and critique between the religious tradition and the psychotherapeutic perspective that is so dominant in American life. Therapeutic practice and psychological theory are themselves immersed in particular "cultures," with value assumptions and ideological commitments that are not necessarily congruent with Christianity. This immersion is not so total that these resources remain useless to the mission of faith. But to use the resources of the culture well, the community of faith must be able to draw upon them critically. Reflective groups, ministers, and theologians must be aware of the assumptions, even biases, from which the paradigms and findings of the social sciences result.[17]   Aware of these limits, the faith community will be better able to dialogue with and to distill the resources of cultural information in the service of the religious mission of justice and meaning.

Notes

1. Michael Cowan, *The Social-Cultural Context of Ministry* (New Orleans: Loyola Institute for Ministry, 1995), p. 22.

2. For an excellent comprehensive review of different approaches to the study of culture, see Robert J. Schreiter, *Constructing Local Theologies* (Maryknoll, NY: Orbis, 1985), pp. 39-74.

3. Clifford Geertz, *The Interpretation of Cultures* (New York: Basic Books, 1973), p. 89.

4. Don Browning, *The Moral Context of Pastoral Care* (Philadelphia: Westminster Press, 1976), p. 73.

5. Avery Dulles has noted Vatican II's cautious suggestion, in its Document on Non-Christian Religions, of the presence of revelation beyond the confines of Christian faith.   Nonbiblical religions are based, in the document's words, on "a certain perception of that hidden power which hovers over the course of things and over the events of human life."   "The events of human life" would include not only religions, but cultures as well.   See pages 100 and following in Dulles' overview of "Faith and Revelation," in *Systematic Theology: Roman Catholic Perspectives*, Francis Schüssler Fiorenza and John P. Galvin, eds. (Minneaplis, MN: Fortress Press, 1991), Vol, I.

6. The conversation about Christianity's relation to culture is long and rich.   Questions raised by Augustine in *City of God* have remained relevant across time, to be taken up again in this century by Paul Tillich in *Theology of Culture* (New York: Oxford University Press, 1959), by Reinhold Niebuhr in *Christ and Culture* (New York: Harper, 1951), and by others. In *Models of Contextual Theology* (Maryknoll, NY: Orbis, 1992), Steven B. Bevins demonstrates both how culture influences theology and how different theologies use culture as a resource.   The work of liberation theologians in Latin America and elsewhere advances a challenging interpretation of Christianity's role in transforming culture; see, for example, Gustavo Gutiérrez, *A Theology of Liberation* (Maryknoll, NY: Orbis, 1973); Juan Luis Segundo, *Liberation of Theology* (Maryknoll, NY: Orbis, 1976); and Maria Pilar Aquino, *Our Cry for Life: Feminist Theology from Latin America* (Maryknoll, NY: Orbis, 1993).

7. Jack Shea, "Doing Ministerial Theology," in David Tracy, ed., *Toward Vatican III* (New York: Seabury, 1978), p. 184.

8. Anne Carr, "Theology and Experience in the Thought of Karl Rahner," *Journal of Religion* 53 (July 1973), p. 373.

9. Browning, *ibid.*

10. For our effort to engage the dialogue between developmental psychology and the categories of a traditional Christian understanding of the human person, see Evelyn Eaton Whitehead and James D. Whitehead, *Christian Life Patterns: The Psychological Challenges and Religious Invitations of Adult Life* (New York: Crossroad, 1992) and *Seasons of Strength: New Visions of Adult Christian Maturing* (Winona, MN: Saint Mary's Press, 1995).

11. We take up the dialogue between contemporary sociology and Christian understandings and aspirations of community in Evelyn Eaton Whitehead and James D. Whitehead, *Community of Faith: Crafting Christian Communities Today* (Mystic, CT: Twenty-Third Publications, 1993).

12. Gregory Baum, *Religion and Alienation* (New York: Paulist Press, 1975), p. 2.

13. For examples of cultural and social analysis as part of theological reflection, see Rebecca Chopp, *The Power to Speak: Feminism, Language, God* (New York: Crossroad, 1991); Joe Holland and Peter Henriot, *Social Analysis: Linking Faith and Justice* (Maryknoll, NY: Orbis, 1984); James E. Hug, ed., *Tracing the Spirit: Communities, Social Action, and Theological Reflection* (New York: Paulist Press, 1983); and John Coleman, *An American Strategic Theology* (New York: Paulist Press, 1982).

14. Andre G. Van Campenhoudt made this observation in his 1975 address to a symposium in the United States on the local church. This address, "Local Churches," is available from *Prospective* in Brussels, Belgium.

15. As an example of the many recent church studies that have taken advantage of sociological research, see J. Gremillion and J. Castelli, *The Emerging Parish: The Notre Dame Study of Catholic Life since Vatican II* (San Francisco, CA: Harper & Row, 1987).

16. Avery Dulles, "Narrowing the Gap: Gospel and Culture," in *Origins*, March 17, 1994 (Vol. 23, No. 39), pp. 677-680.

17. Browning, *ibid.*; see also his *A Fundamental Practical Theology: Descriptive and Strategic Proposals* (Minneapolis: Augsburg Fortress, 1991).

• Part III •

A Method for Theological Reflection in Ministry

The conversation that is reflection in ministry moves from listening to mutual assertion to pastoral response.

Attending is a Christian virtue through which we patiently discern the voice of God wherever revealed. This virtue encompasses a range of specific skills—from the ability to read accurately a scriptural text, to the patience to discern the movements of our own heart, to the ability to listen carefully to the movement of the Spirit in the faith community.

Listening to the Word, we are called to witness to it. Our witnessing brings us into the embrace of other believers. This communal exploration of the testimony of Christian tradition, personal experience, and cultural insight can be described as assertion.

The lively assertion of experience and insight bears fruit in faithful action. Thus, in a movement of pastoral response the faith community expresses its conviction in service to and transformation of the world.

In Part Three we examine this dynamic of theological reflection through which the ministering community moves from experience to insight to action.

· 5 ·

Attending:
The Conversation Begins

Incline your ear, and come to me;
Listen, so that you may live.
I will make with you an everlasting covenant.
(Isaiah 55:3)

ATTENDING TO GOD'S PRESENCE IS THE INITIAL STANCE OF CHRISTIAN
faith. The covenant, Isaiah suggests, is contingent on this receptive
posture: "Listen, so that you may live." Pastoral reflection, too, begins in listening. Whatever the challenge a faith community faces, its
spiritual discernment begins in paying close attention to what the
religious heritage, the surrounding culture, and the members' experience have to say. The model reminds the group that it must listen
carefully to the various, often conflicting, information arising from
these three sources.

But listening is difficult. Paying attention to one another—or
even to the stirrings in our own heart—is seldom easy. Fatigued or
depressed, we show up for an important meeting, only to find our
attention wavering as others express their ideas and convictions. Or
we arrive in an antagonistic mood; as our adversary speaks we busy
ourselves rehearsing a rejoinder. Absorbed in our own response, we
have no space to really listen to another person. Or, already convinced that our vision is the only proper view of things, we have no
need to honor other people's contribution. These examples remind
us that attending is a learned discipline, a virtue.

Communities of faith today, and especially their ministers, are
searching for ways to develop this spiritual discipline. Contemporary believers are more acutely aware of themselves as *seekers* than

as *possessors* of truth and grace. Such modesty has long been an insight (if not always a practice) in the Christian tradition. The increased visibility of other faith traditions, coupled with profound changes experienced within Protestant, Orthodox, and Catholic churches alike, make us more conscious of our status as learners. We are called to listen continually and carefully to God's surprising presence in human history.

This shift in self-understanding deeply affects the style of ministerial leadership. The religious leader today is seen less exclusively as the one who *brings* God and more as one who helps *discern* God, already present. The minister is a skillful attendant to the movements of God wherever these appear. The word *attendant* captures well this shift in the stance of Christian leadership. Ministry is moving away from a more authoritative and hierarchical style in which a minister is one who molds and rules. The shift is toward a style of servant leadership in which the minister is an attendant—one whose role is to listen for the Lord's presence and to assist other believers in their attentive response to God's movement in their lives.[1]

This vision of religious leadership requires of ministers a new self-definition and a new asceticism, as their central role in the community of faith is seen as including a capacity for creative listening to complement the traditionally more highlighted roles of preacher, judge, decision-maker.

In the New Testament the virtue of obedience is rooted in the word for listening (*akouein*). This word, in turn, echoes the modern English word "acoustics." The acoustics of a space are the properties that help us hear. Just as the acoustics in an auditorium may be poor, making it difficult to understand the speaker, the spiritual acoustics in a community may be muddled as well, making it difficult for us to listen to one another.

Religious leaders at times find themselves in communities where misunderstanding and mistrust distort the conversation. Whatever its cause—hostility or apathy or fear—the distortion undermines the group's spiritual life. A mature faith community manifests obedience in its disciplined willingness to pay attention to one another. As theologian Paul Philibert observes, "the obedience of mature Christian adults is primarily a community listening carefully for the signs of the Spirit, rather than one individual submitting to another invididual."[2]

This understanding of obedience asks something different of religious leaders—to see to the acoustics of the group. Less and less is their task to provide answers; more and more they serve by improving the conditions of our common life so that we can truly hear one another. By supporting the faith community in this privileged conversation, ministers attune us to the murmurs of the Spirit in our midst.

To listen well does not mean to accept all comments without criticism; it does not demand "man on the street interviews" in which every random observation is given equal weight. Obedient listening acknowledges that the privileged metaphors of Scripture and the established roles of formal leaders merit special attention. But Christians remember that our Scripture reveals a God who speaks in surprising ways—in the cries of the poor and dispossessed, and in questions raised by outsiders and nonbelievers. Religious obedience requires our attentiveness to these unlikely voices as well.

Interpersonal Skills of Attending

To most of us, listening well comes neither as a native ability nor as a special gift. Instead, we must *learn* better ways to attend to one another and to our experience of faith. Over the past several decades, the fields of psychology and the management sciences have contributed to a clearer understanding of communication skills.[3] In this chapter and the next, we will examine the skills required for effective interpersonal communication and then explore the relevance of these attitudes and behaviors for the larger conversation that is theological reflection in ministry.

The skill of attending begins in active patience. To listen, we must hold ourself still enough to hear. Paying attention like this is a receptive but not a passive stance. Attending well opens us to the full context of the conversation—the words and silences, the emotions and ideas, the situation in which the conversation takes place. But listening does not end in this openness. Its object and its proof is that we respond with understanding, that is, with both accuracy (I have heard correctly what you have said) and with empathy (I appreciate its meaning, its significance to you).

The two basic components of attending are thus the ability to listen actively and the ability to respond with accurate understanding. Skills of active listening are those which enable us to be aware of the full message. So we pay attention to the words that are spoken. But non-verbal factors are equally important—posture, tone of voice, eye contact, timing, gestures, emotional nuance. In written communication, too, context shapes the full message. The tone of the writing (scholarly or popular, argumentative or conciliatory, analytic or inspirational), the format in which it appears (there are crucial differences among a handwritten note, a printed flyer, and an engraved invitation), the timing of its publication—all these may reveal information of as much significance as the words we read.

To listen actively, then, calls for an awareness of the content, feeling, and context of communication.

Responding accurately also requires a range of skills. First among these is empathy—the ability to understand another person's ideas, feelings, and values from within that person's frame of reference. Empathy does not mean agreement; it does not require that I accept the other's point of view as my own or even as "best" or "right" for that person. The goal of empathy is to understand; as such it precedes evaluation. Evaluation and decision are not necessarily secondary in communication, but they follow on accurate understanding.

A second skill for accurate response is paraphrasing. I show that I understand your meaning by saying back to you the essence of your message. To paraphrase is not merely to parrot, to repeat mechanically what you have just said. The goal is to show that I have really heard *you*, not just your words but their wider significance. Restating what I have understood also honors your communication. Now you can confirm my response or clarify your meaning. In either case, I demonstrate my respect for what you have to say.

We have thus far discussed these skills of attending in terms of their use in personal communication. But their relevance in ministry and pastoral reflection goes beyond the strictly interpersonal situation. The model of reflection we discuss here calls the minister and the community of faith to the use of these skills in pastoral decision making. Let us examine now how these skills are relevant to the processes of theological reflection in ministry.

Attending in Theological Reflection

> Beloved, do not believe every spirit, but test the spirits
> to see whether they are from God. (1 John 4:1)

Skillful listening begins the process of spiritual discernment. From St. Paul to Ignatius Loyola to contemporary spiritual direction, Christians have been concerned to carefully discern what forces are at play in the important decisions of our lives. Moral theologian William Spohn describes this discernment as "the graced ability to detect how the person should respond to the invitation of God in this concrete situation."[4]

In theological reflection in ministry this "testing of the spirits" begins in attending to the information available in each of the three sources in pastoral reflection. In a reflective community, members must attend well to their own experience—in both the personal and professional spheres. Attending here is part of the lifelong process of self-knowledge and self-acceptance which marks both maturity and holiness. Such self-awareness is the basis of that gradually developing confidence in our own, admittedly partial, experience of faith. This maturity includes a recognition of, even comfort with, the ambiguities of one's interior life. Knowing the contradictions and confusions—as well as the convictions—of our own soul helps us stand with others in their pain and doubt and joy. Coming to this mellow, even peaceful, awareness of how unfinished is our own grasp of truth leaves us less defensive in the face of new or challenging information. We stand more open to the truth that may reside, half-hidden, in our own or others' ongoing experience.

This openness touches Christian spirituality. Feeling less need to fill periods of prayer with words and images, we may adopt a more receptive stance, attempting rather to empty the heart and "wait on the Lord." Or we may find that keeping a personal journal attunes us to the movement of the Spirit in our life. These and other efforts to listen within are, we would argue, basic tools for a reflective ministry.

The attitudes and skills of attending enable us to learn from the experiences of others as well as from our own. Approaching a person in ministry, our first response is to listen well—for the word which God has already spoke here, for the word of gift or need that the person brings, for the word of challenge or confirmation that this person's experience holds for the religious tradition. The communication skills of attentive posture, sensitive paraphrasing, and empathic response enhance our presence and performance in the myriad interpersonal situations of ministry—preaching and teaching, counseling and consoling, advocacy and planning, problem solving and conflict resolution. Our personal and communal experience, well attended, carries religious information to illumine our pastoral response.

Christian ministers are challenged today to develop attending skills not only at the personal level, but also in regard to religious tradition and culture. Academic theology has become enormously more sophisticated in this century in its means of accurately attending to the sources of the Christian tradition. The art and science of hermeneutics remind us that the interpretation of any document begins in critically attending to both text and context. In biblical studies, text criticism and form criticism alert us to the significance of the various contexts, the "life situations" in which the sacred texts were composed. Historians of Christianity teach the minister, likewise, to attend to the decisions of Chalcedon, Augsburg, and Trent and to the cultural contexts of these ecclesial events. The reflective minister must also be able, in a more immediate setting, to discern the signs of the times (an imperative we discussed in Chapter Four) and to attend effectively to "the sense of the faithful," this community's grasp of the tradition (as we saw in Chapters One and Three).

The third source to which a minister must attend is the culture as it speaks in various voices: the media, the social sciences, the dominant cultural philosophy, the technology it prizes. Reflective communities pay attention to these cultural sources, expecting to find information that will influence pastoral decision making and even, in grace, to hear the word that the Lord speaks in this cultural context. Not every minister will be comfortable in dialogue with each of these cultural sources. Not every pastoral decision will require or benefit from information from each source. But the process of theological reflection in ministry will characteristically include information drawn from cultural sources. And the reflective minister will expect to develop some degree of personal competence in approaching the sources of cultural information.

Theologian Jack Shea discusses four ways in which the dynamic of listening and response is a part of the theological responsibility of contemporary ministers.[5] Many people today have only nonreligious language in which to speak of their ultimate questions and experiences. Ministers, then, need to be able to hear the religious themes imbedded in the secular vocabulary of the age—the cultural discussions of personal development, of justice and political reform, of ecological concern, of artistic expression, of belonging and community. They need to recognize and respond to these religious experiences implicit in apparently secular concerns, sensitive to the ways in which these correspond to the traditional images in which Christianity has understood itself.

Second, ministers are called upon today to assist the larger community of faith in its transition from one theological self-understanding to another. In the Catholic community this is often seen (though, no doubt, too simplistically) as the movement from a pre-Vatican II to a postconciliar theology. Similar transitions are being experienced in many Protestant and Orthodox communities as well. To assist these transitions ministers will need to listen well to the explicit religious questions (often expressed in the categories of an earlier theology) that arise among believers, to discern the deeper values of faith that these questions touch, and to respond in a manner that reflects both theological accuracy and respect for the tradition which grounds the question.

Third, the minister must be able to hear the assumptions and presuppositions that lie behind the religious programs and pastoral decisions that are currently in effect. Alert to these underlying categories, even prejudices, of thought and value, the minister can assist a community of believers to come to more critical awareness of the frame of reference which guides their actions. These assumptions can then be examined in the light of the gospel and subsequently reinforced or altered, so that the faith community's actions are consonant with its deepest understanding of its mission.

The fourth listening task of ministry today, as Shea sees it, is to discern this ongoing relationship between faith and action. What are the creative links between the Christian story and the concrete activities—individual initiatives and institutional decisions—which the community of faith undertakes in the world? If the third listening task invites a critical examination of the current "established" shape of ministry, this fourth invites an equally critical exploration of the new forms of Christian action that may be demanded as the church moves into its future.

Attending as a Ministerial Asceticism

Our emphasis on attending as part of the pastoral reflection process can be described in terms of a religious discipline or asceticism. The skilled attentiveness in which reflection begins and on which it is grounded is itself an exercise in self-emptying. As Jesus Christ "empties himself, taking the form of a servant" (Philippians 2:7), ministers skilled in pastoral reflection empty themselves to allow space for revelation. Such a movement of emptying applies whether the person is attending to a scriptural text, a social movement, or stirrings within an individual's life. This spirituality of *kenosis* (emptiness), little emphasized in an action-and-achievement-oriented culture such as ours, is required of every Christian. Such a spirituality, we have suggested, is exercised not only in prayer, but in the specific, learned behaviors through which we can more effectively empty ourselves of our own agenda at the first stage of a reflection. "Our agenda" here includes those convictions and prejudices, hopes and distractions, which usually accompany us and can short-circuit the reflective process.

A significant part of the challenge of attending, whether to a text or to another person, is suspending interpretation and judgment until we have thoroughly *heard*. Knowing in advance what this text *must* mean or what *this kind* of person needs, we fail to listen fully. When prior interpretations limit our listening, these prejudgments function as prejudice.

A special maturity is demanded in such ascetical attending. Listeners must have sufficient self-trust and self-confidence to set themselves aside for a time. Such maturity allows us to listen nondefensively, relatively empty of our own needs and preconceptions and genuinely open to the new and unexpected.

The spiritual discipline required for skillful pastoral attending must be supported by an ascetical life style—a way of living and working that does not *regularly* find us overcommitted. The hectic life style of many of us today imperils pastoral reflection. Our busyness fosters fatigue and distraction, inhibits skillful listening, and disrupts effective reflection. Pastoral reflection, then, carries implications not only for ministerial education but for spirituality and personal maturity as well.

Finally, the spiritual disciplines that support effective listening can help ministers deal with the expectation (among one's parishioners and within oneself) that the minister be the "knower"—official spokesperson for the faith community, one who has the answers and can take a stand. Such a role is, in part, appropriate to the religious leader. But ministers today must complement this representative role with the skills of communal discernment, which stress listening, receptivity, and shared responsibility in discovering God's actions among us. Increased skill at attending to God's movements will help ministers be more comfortable with their own partial knowledge, more alert to "the signs of the times," and better attendants to the Christian community.

Notes

1. In the 1980s the American Catholic bishops sponsored an invigorating discussion throughout the country on the role of women in church life. In 140 dioceses more than 75,000 enjoyed the opportunity to be heard. A first draft of a pastoral letter, entitled "Partners in the Mystery of Redemption," demonstrated the fruit of this listening; a large percent of the letter was contributions by women. But the letter met stiff resistance in Rome. A second draft edited out most of the women's witness as well as the central metaphor of partnership. A third draft and then a fourth draft drifted further from the energy of the originating reflection. Engulfed in disagreement and disappointment, the project was finally shelved.

Bishop P. Francis Murphy of Baltimore, in an evaluation of the failed effort, summarized the central objection of Vatican officials to the listening process itself: "They asserted that bishops are teachers, not learners; truth cannot emerge through consultation." But Bishop Murphy also noted that, even in defeat, an important and irreversible change in the bishops' style of reflection had been made: "The real strength of the process is that the bishops' committee listened to a diversity of women who are members of the church's body. It consulted the experience of many whose talents and aspirations are unjustly overlooked, especially in the church."

For the first draft of the pastoral letter, entitled "Partners in the Mystery of Redemption," see *Origins* (the documentary service of the National Conference of Catholic Bishops), April 21, 1988, pp. 757-88. See Bishop Murphy's remarks on the failed nine year process in "Let's Start Over: A Bishop Appraises the Pastoral on Women," *Commonweal*, Sept. 25, 1992, p. 12.

2. See Paul Philibert's remarks in his "Readiness for Ritual: Psychological Aspects of Maturity in Christian Celebration," in Regis Duffy, ed., *Alternate Futures For Worship*, Vol. I (Collegeville, MN: Liturgical Press, 1987), p. 115. We explore the changing shape of obedience in a maturing church in Chapter 16 of *The Promise of Partnership: A Model for Collaborative Ministry* (HarperSanFrancisco, 1993) and in Chapter 12 of *Seasons of Strength: New Visions of Adult Christian Maturing* (Winona, MN: Saint Mary's Press, 1995).

3. Psychologist Gerard Egan has pioneered a practical approach to training in listening skills. See, for example, his *The Skilled Helper: A Model for Systematic Helping and Interpersonal Relating* (Monterey, CA: Brooks/Cole, 1991. Also see Robert Bolton's *People Skills: How to Assert Yourself, Listen to Others, and Resolve Conflict* (New York: Touchstone Books, 1986). Thomas Hart applies the skills of listening to Christian spirituality in his excellent *The Art of Christian Listening* (Mahwah, NJ: Paulist Press, 1981).

4. See William Spohn's discussion of discernment and "the reasoning heart" in "Christian Discernment of the Nuclear Issue," in *New Catholic World*, Nov./Dec., 1983, pp. 262-66. We are grateful to our colleague Corita Clark for her observations on the links between our method of pastoral reflection and the tradition of Christian discernment; see her *A Spirituality for Active Ministry* (Kansas City: Sheed & Ward, 1991).

5. See Jack Shea's "Doing Ministerial Theology," in D. Tracy, ed., *Toward Vatican III* (New York: Seabury Press, 1978), pp. 188-95. Shea's creative style of theological reflection is displayed in his *An Experience Named Spirit* (Chicago, IL: Thomas More Press, 1983) and *The Spirit Master* (Chicago, IL: Thomas More Press, 1987).

· 6 ·

The Crucible of Assertion

THE CONVERSATION THAT IS PASTORAL REFLECTION BEGINS AS WE PAY close attention to significant voices both past and present. On any pastoral question—reconciliation or leadership or liturgy—we are likely to hear contending accounts. Scripture itself often includes conflicting testimony. Bringing these differing voices into dialogue moves the conversation to a new stage. This stage of mutual engagement requires *assertion* at both the theological and interpersonal levels.

A faith community at this stage struggles with the tensions generated by the diversity it has uncovered. Frequently confusion and anxiety result—both for individuals and for the group. Having a workable method helps by providing a structure for honest confrontation among differing views and values.

The challenge for leaders and other members is to help shape a holding environment—a gathering where it is safe to admit our doubts and to acknowledge our differences. A reflective community provides a protective space where we can explore the truth and tolerate the ambiguity of our ignorance. Such a setting functions as a sanctuary, a privileged place where prayerful conversation happens. Without this mood of safety and tolerance, confronting complex issues of faith and justice is daunting.

A Holding Environment

The term *holding environment* has special significance in the work of British psychologist D. W. Winnicott.[1] Looking at factors that help children thrive, Winnicott studied the common family setting of a small child absorbed in play while the mother is working nearby. Fascinated by the youngster's wrapt attention, Winnicott describes the child as "alone in the presence of another." Intellectual and emotional growth seems to require this paradoxical context, where the child is alone (absorbed in his own activities) and not alone (a nearby presence protects his vulnerability). Winnicott's research shows that an environment like this richly supports the child's development. In such a setting, children learn to concentrate, to take risks, to grow toward independent judgment.

What supports development here? The parent's presence signals safety, so that the child feels free to explore her world. The parent's non-interference expands the freedom, encouraging the child to trust her experience and welcome surprise.

"Being alone in the presence of another" seems an apt description of a reflective community. Struggling to sustain the assertive stance of *faith seeking understanding*, a group may feel off-balance. Sensing we are "on our own" in new ways, still we know we are not abandoned. The promise of God's abiding Spirit—even within *this* community, blessed and broken—steadies us at this stage. When diversity surfaces and disagreement threatens, a parental leader may be tempted to intervene, undermining the group's development by outlawing conflict or smoothing over differences. But experienced leaders acknowledge their responsibility to nurture the holding environment, helping the group welcome pluralism as a potential ally and befriend conflict as a necessary embrace.

Assertion's challenge, both interpersonally and theologically, is to find a balance by which we can present our own insights and beliefs forcefully, without forcing them on others. Two characteristics of the contemporary life of faith underscore the importance of assertiveness in pastoral reflection. The first is a keen awareness of religious pluralism. More and more today we realize that the differences between our beliefs and those of others are not simply the result of ignorance or deceit. The pluralism we experience among us reveals the real but partial access that each of us has to the truth. As we saw in Chapter Two, biblical scholars and church historians remind us that this pluralism is not just a contemporary phenomenon. The Christian witness of faith has been pluriform since the beginning, its diversity a sign both of the richness of its good news and the inexplicable mystery of God.

In the face of this religious pluralism—both within and beyond each community of faith—skills of assertion become especially crucial. Genuine religious dialogue can occur only when our values and beliefs are shared honestly and respectfully with those whose lives are guided by other religious insights and convictions. Ecumenical dialogue is vitiated when participants can maintain neither a truly attentive nor an assertive posture. Dialogue requires more than stating our truth, pausing politely, and then restating it. Dialogue in this latter mode functions not as a mutual exploration, but as an attempt—usually fruitless—at indoctrination.

A second characteristic of the contemporary life of faith reinforces the need for assertion. Christian maturity invites us to grow into the full adulthood of Jesus Christ. We remain children of God all our lives, celebrating our origins in God's love and our continuing dependence on God's graciousness. Yet participating as adult believers expands our sense of responsibility in the community of faith. Maturing as Christians, we recognize that we are more than simply heirs of the tradition, more than simply recipients of its gifts. We are called to share in handing on the faith. This responsibility places us in a more assertive relationship to the tradition itself.

Religious maturity compels us to engage our religious heritage at a deeper level, where its inconsistencies and contradictions become painfully clear. For many believers, paradoxically, grappling with the insitution's historical and current frailties results in a deeper appreciation of the tradition's vitality and its continuing contribution to the human community.

Reaching this mature stance in faith requires an adult relationship with God. Adult faith demands a searching and challenging response to God's ambiguous presence in our lives. The biblical story of Jacob wrestling with Yahweh offers a model. To struggle and contest with God is, to be sure, to enter into a threatening relationship. Religious assertiveness, a virtue gradually developed in adult life, gives us courage to stay with the struggle "to the breaking of the day." With this strength of religious maturity we are able to wait upon the Lord's presence without falling into either extreme—a childish passivity or a rebellious rejection. In this sense, assertiveness is both a skill required for theological reflection and a necessary virtue of Christian maturity.

Reimagining Conflict

The story of Jacob wrestling with God gives us an important clue to the dynamic of the stage of assertion. A community's conversation will be fruitful only if we can picture disagreement, dissent and conflict as potentially positive dynamics in our shared life.[2]

Jacob's experience reminds us that conflict is one of the ways we hold people whom we love; it is an honorable embrace. Those of us who have learned simply to be scandalized by disagreement find this view of conflict unsettling. We listen again to Jacob's story, attentive to the clues it holds for the community of faith today. In the darkness, Jacob struggles with an unknown adversary. Jacob is beset, confused; he sustains serious injury. Yet in this struggle, through the struggle, Jacob and his antagonist find their way to a new, richer relationship. Both participants are changed: Jacob's identity is so significantly altered that his name is changed to Israel; Yahweh is forced to surrender a blessing. In the faith community, too, our differences often bring us into conflict. In the struggle, we sustain both wounds and transformations. The struggle itself seems to be part of the transforming process, the path along which both revelation and reconciliation lie. Always turning away from controversy, simply refusing to engage our differences, seldom leads to peace. Instead we settle for a superficial calm.

The gospel, too, includes stories of conflict. Jesus' parables—indeed, his life—show us that conflict is part of the plot. Parables overthrow our certainties and our confident orthodoxy; an agonizing personal struggle reveals new and surprising parts of ourself. We can, in fact, trace the long history of the Christian tradition by tracking the debates and disagreements that have energized and shaped our common life. As philosopher Alisdair McIntyre observes, "traditions, when vital, embody continuities of conflict."[3]

But Christian piety has been especially reluctant to celebrate this truth. Many of us have learned that in religious matters disagreement signals disloyalty and dissent is equal to disobedience. We have sought to replace the embrace of conflict with a virtue of docility. But the vital disagreements that energize the church today teach us again the painful lesson: conflict is part of the plot. Reimagining conflict as an honorable embrace, we struggle to craft a virtue of assertion to serve the faith community today.

Assertion as an Interpersonal Skill

An ability to insert ourselves effectively into the larger world in which we live is a sign of adult maturity.[4] The capacity for engagement is key to success in love and work, in cooperation and conflict. This ability for mature interaction psychologists call assertiveness. Being assertive means reaching out to other people—starting a project, offering help, expressing an idea, or defending our rights. Assertion marks many of the ordinary transactions of daily life: we invite a friend to join us for lunch; we close the door to keep out noise from an adjoining room; we call to correct a computer error in a bank statement; we suggest a plan for how our ministry team might proceed. In each case, we take some personal action that influences our world or shapes our environment.

But disagreement and conflict are the real test of an assertive stance. Confronted by conflict, nonassertive people either refuse to speak or too readily give in, letting others have their way. Aggressive people try to insure that their own position wins out. An assertive attitude permits more flexibility. There will be circumstances in which an assertive person will set aside his or her position; there may be other times when assertion demands holding firmly to a position even in the face of valid and significant opposition. But the more characteristic assertive stance is to acknowledge the validity of both positions and to negotiate toward some mutually acceptable resolution, one which respects the core values of both parties even as it requires mutual accommodation.

An assertive attitude, then, involves self-awareness, self-disclosure, and self-worth. *Self-awareness* puts us in touch with the dense and ambiguous information of our own life. This knowledge is not likely to be full and finished; one indication of a nonassertive stance, in fact, is an unwillingness to act until we are completely sure.

Self-disclosure means we are able to express ourselves in appropriate ways. Pastoral reflection, for example, does not demand the intimacy of close friends, but it does require that we be able to describe our experience, share our vision, tell one another what we think and how we feel about issues that touch our common life. To communicate our ideas and values, we must have the words that help us be understood. This brings us to the question of vocabulary. In some situations in ministry, for example, using theological terms correctly may be of critical importance to expressing ourselves accurately. A lay volunteer in ministry, for example, wants to speak of her work in explicitly theological terms so that its pastoral relevance can be better appreciated by herself and others in the church. On the other hand, to share ourself with a close friend we need a nuanced vocabulary of feelings, one that goes well beyond "I feel good" and "I feel bad."[5] Other vocabularies help us be effective in the tasks of our particular ministry—as a preacher or chaplain or pastoral planner. We strengthen assertiveness by expressing ourselves in ways that fit the different settings of our personal and professional lives.

Being clear and concrete when we speak also helps assertion. When we retreat into generalities, for example, saying "everybody knows. . ." instead of "I think that . . ."; or "people have a hard time . . ." instead of "it is difficult for me . . . .", communication stalls. Assertion often requires that I speak in the first person, learning to say "I," to acknowledge my own ideas and needs and values.

Speaking concretely means providing details. For example, saying "things are going well for me in the parish" communicates some information, but not very much. Communication goes further when we share specifics of the situation: "Over the past months I worked closely with the officers of the parish council in planning a lay leadership retreat that they conducted last weekend. I enjoyed the give and take of the planning sessions and I felt good about being able to work with them as peers in the retreat itself." Again, saying "I really feel discouraged in my ministry" is a start. But this self-disclosure becomes more concrete when we describe the discouraging events.

Self-worth helps us be assertive. Beyond knowing our insights, needs, and purposes, we must value them. Assertiveness doesn't demand that we judge our own ideas as always the best. Rather we judge our experience as deserving of consideration and respect—from ourself and from others as well. Our perceptions have worth and weight. By valuing them, we help others appreciate them too.

Additional skills help us sustain an assertive dialogue. Being able to tolerate the ambiguity that arises as we attempt to hold several perspectives in tension is crucial. Effective assertion also requires some ease in facing conflict. But, as we saw earlier, a religious interpretation of conflict simply as scandal undermines this difficult embrace.

Facing conflict begins in the realization that conflict is normal and in the conviction that it need not always work against our shared purpose. Managing conflict successfully requires skills of confrontation. Confrontation here means more than hostile interpersonal exchange. Skills of confrontation enable use to give and receive emotionally significant information in ways that invite further exploration rather than self-defense. To confront effectively, we need to communicate in nonjudgmental ways, to deal with anger in ourselves and others, and to offer emotional support even as we disagree. These interpersonal skills carry over into the dialogue which marks theological reflection in ministry.

Assertion as a Stage in Theological Reflection

When we have carefully attended to the information arising from tradition, culture, and our own experience, we must bring the information into contact. This encounter may be a relatively peaceful one in which insights confirm and further illumine each other. But often the engagement becomes tense and challenging. Whatever the style of encounter, the success of this reflection depends on each source being allowed to assert its claims.

The conversation instigated at the assertion stage supposes some mutuality among the partners. This mutuality is not a strict equality; the Christian tradition and its information enjoy a position of privilege and priority in theological reflection. As Christians we believe that this revelation, even as shaped by centuries of interpretations and misuse, is normative: here we encounter the story of God's loving presence in human history. Yet the tradition, as we have seen, is itself the fruit of an ongoing and often conflicted conversation: Scripture as interpreted by believers in particular historical and cultural contexts; historical developments guided by God's unfailing presence and shaped by fallible human decisions. Karl Rahner's formula for the theologian's twofold task—to recover and to overcome—highlights the ambiguity of the assertive stage of reflection. In a reflection in which cultural and personal influences on a specific concern are acknowledged and in which the plural interpretations of a rich and varied religious heritage are attended to, the assertion stage provides the occasion for recovering and overcoming the tradition. Whether we are addressing questions of social justice (and contemporary forms of slavery and oppression) or of denominational life (and the changing role of the laity), the assertion stage brings traditional religious formulations under review. In this model, tradition is seen neither as merely a human product nor as an undiluted divine deposit. The interplay of divine and human in our religious heritage makes ongoing pastoral reflection both necessary and exciting.

The benefit for contemporary ministry of actively engaging all three sources is clear when we consider the alternatives.

A reflection in which tradition simply interprets experience, without consideration of cultural information (whether through neglect of the exegetical sciences on the interpretation of Scripture or of psychological understanding of the human person) leads us toward fundamentalism. A reflection that limits the dialogue to cultural information and individual experience is not explicitly Christian. Finally, a reflection which is essentially a dialogue between the Christian tradition and cultural information (whether philosophy, philology, or science), to the neglect of personal experience, tends to yield conclusions of a more theoretical nature. Since the experience of participants is overlooked, the pastoral conclusions arising from such a reflection are often abstract or simply irrelevant.

We can note other ways in which the mutuality necessary for theological reflection can be lost. A community can be so influenced by personal experience (as, for example, its awareness of the patriarchal and misogynist tendencies in the history and current life of the church) that it feels forced to reject the tradition. Overwhelmed by these negative experiences, the group is unable to explore the tradition's other (and sometimes contradictory) testimony on women, personal worth, and human liberation. Here the conversation concerning women and Christianity breaks off.

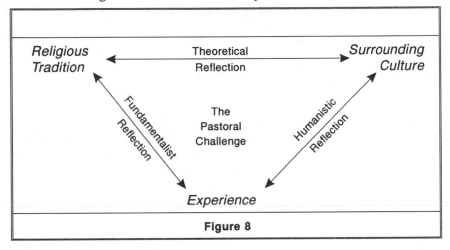

Figure 8

But the dialogue can be broken in other ways as well. A community may be so impressed with a teaching drawn from the tradition (as, for example, official Vatican decrees on the moral evil of contraception) that the testimony of mature married Catholics—their experiences of marriage, sexuality, and parenthood—seem irrelevant. Assertive dialogue is not possible in such a situation. Attending only to one source of information (tradition) and crediting only part of the information available there (focusing exclusively on the statements concerning contraception and neglecting the tradition's conviction of the importance of personal conscience), the reflection fails.

In our first example it is experience that disrupts the assertive conversation of theological reflection. In the second, tradition functions in that role. Culture, too, can be an aggressor in theological reflection, especially when its influence goes unrecognized. A powerful and painful example of this is found in the history of Christian missions. For centuries well-intentioned European and North American missionaries brought with them not only the gospel but Western cultural values and prejudices as well. Only recently have we become aware of the cultural imperialism implicit in many of our best missionary efforts. If the unwitting influence of cultural biases has undercut many of our missionary efforts, the contemporary awareness of this influence awakens a more careful reflection on how the good news of the gospel can be proclaimed to all peoples.

We began this chapter with a discussion of two factors in contemporary Christian life that highlight the need for assertion in theological reflection today: our growing awareness of religious pluralism and the increasing maturity of Christian faithful. A third factor is significant as well: the understanding of ministry as a corporate endeavor, a task shared within the community of faith. When the minister stands alone, in an autonomous role as sole authoritative leader within the community, there is less need for attitudes of assertion and skills of interaction. In such a setting, conflict must appear as disobedience. But when, as today, the reflections and decisions that shape the Christian community are seen as necessarily collective, as growing out of and respecting a shared experience of faith, assertion becomes a crucial virtue. This virtue and its attendant skills stand at the heart of the processes of pastoral response, to which we now turn.

Notes

1. D. W. Winnicott explores the imagery of "a holding environment" throughout his work; see, for instance, his *Playing and Reality* (London: Tavistock, 1971). English psychotherapist Adam Phillips offers exciting expansions of Winnicott's image in his *On Kissing, Tickling, and Being Bored* (Cambridge, MA: Harvard University Press, 1993).

2. We explore the dynamic of conflict in ministry in *The Promise of Partnership: A Model for Collaborative Ministry* (HarperSanFrancisco, 1993); see Chapters 4, 8, and 15.

3. See p. 206 of Alisdair MacIntyre's *After Virtue* (Notre Dame, IN: Notre Dame Press, 1981).

4. Robert Alberti and Michael Emmons and their colleagues at Impact Publishers have made important contributions to the literature of assertion theory and skills. Their early work, *Your Perfect Right: A Guide to Assertive Behavior* (San Luis Obispo, CA: Impact, 1974) remains a classic on the topic. Since then, Alberti has edited *Assertiveness: Innovations, Applications, Issues* (1977) and Stanlee Phelps and Nancy Austin have published their influential *The Assertive Woman* (1975), both published at Impact.

Neil Katz and John W. Lawyer provide a useable guide to the practical skills of conflict negotiation in *Conflict Resolution: Building Bridges* (Newbury Park, CA: Corwin Press, 1993). In *Managing Church Conflict* (Philadelphia: Westminster, 1991), Hugh Halverstadt provides practical gound rules for dealing effectively with conflict in religious groups. Doris Donnelly gives graceful insight into the tasks of personal and communal reconciliation in *Putting Forgiveness into Practice* (Nashville: Abingdon Press, 1986).

5. We explore the disciplines of naming the emotions in *Shadows of the Heart: A Spirituality of the Negative Emotions* (New York: Crossroad, 1994).

• 7 •

Pastoral Response:
From Insight to Action

THE PURPOSE OF THEOLOGICAL REFLECTION IN MINISTRY IS "TO ALLOW faith perspectives to influence personal and social life."[1] Pastoral reflection seeks not religious insight alone, but insightful religious action. The reflective process leads us to deeper appreciation of the religious heritage and the ambiguous power of its symbols in the faith community today. This deeper appreciation is a "traditioned awareness" out of which faithful action can flow. So the critical test of reflection *in ministry* is not simply the quality of the insight to which it leads but the quality of the pastoral response which is its fruit.

We turn now to the third stage of the method, where communal decision making advances the community's commitment to effective pastoral response. To be sure, throughout the reflective process decisions have been required and choices have been made: what issues to consider, what sources to consult, who will be involved in the conversation. At this final stage, decision making names the practical strategies that move the community from shared insight to joint response.

Over the fifteen years since our initial work on this pastoral method, churches have been blessed with the appearance of a rich array of practical approaches to communal decision making and action planning. In *Sharing Wisdom: A Guide to Being and Building Church*, for example, Mary Benet McKinney describes the proven procedure for group decision making that she has used widely in Catholic settings. Kennon Callahan's tested program of congregational renewal, available in his Effective Church Leadership Series, has served many Protestant parishes. So faith communities and their religious leaders today are familiar with strategies to develop mission statements, clarify ministry goals, evaluate pastoral programs, remedy poor performance, and celebrate successes achieved. And many denominations provide staff consultants and other resources to assist local communities in their planning efforts.[2]

Our goal here is not to suggest a singular action plan as stage three of the method or to prescribe one particular strategy of communal discernment as appropriate for all groups. Our own experience reinforces the conviction of pastoral leaders and reflective communities: there are *many right ways* to bring shared insight to fruition in effective common response. In Part Four of this book we include examples of the work of several colleagues, each offering a tested perspective on how pastoral reflection informs pastoral action.

In this chapter we offer one example, drawn from our own ministry as pastoral consultants, of a reflective community moving through listening and assertion toward practical pastoral response. Here, as in most instances, the model/method serves best when it functions as a flexible guide rather than as a rigid program to which the group process must conform.[3]

A Diocese Plans for the Future

The Director of On-going Formation for Priests, himself a pastor, contacted us for assistance. He spoke as a member of a five person planning team (two priests, a woman religious, and two lay persons) commissioned by the recent diocesan synod, its responsibility to advance the synod's call for greater collaboration in ministry throughout the diocese. The planning group contracted with us to work with them through the first phase of their mandate, to culminate in a diocesan-wide conference.

1. Listening and Assertion

Early discussions with the planning group led to a decision to survey those who minister in the diocese, to gather information about the current state of shared ministry. A simple survey guide was developed and mailed to priests, religious and lay persons serving in leadership capacity in pastoral service. Respondents to the survey listed successes and failures at working together in parishes and other church institutions. They frequently noted the different and sometimes conflicting attitudes towards working together: are the non-ordained simply "helping out the pastor" or are they genuine partners in this effort? Respondents expressed an enthusiasm for a new mood of cooperation they found in the diocese, and also a recurrent disillusionment when efforts of cooperation foundered. Many respondents cited a troubling pattern: in the face of conflict some pastors seemed to abandon their aspirations toward partnership in ministry and revert to old, authoritarian styles of decision making. Even apart from these conflicted situations, some respondents complained that they were frequently included in the early discussion of a planning process but regularly excluded from later stages of decision making. Others noted that while the rhetoric of collaboration was strong, traditional structures of authority still meant that a lay director of religious education or other pastoral worker in the parish could be summarily fired by the pastor, without cause or appeal. The survey results showed that hope for genuine collaboration in ministry in the diocese was high, but so was the experience of conflicting ecclesial visions.

2. Decision

After studying the responses, the planning team decided that the culminating conference should take the form of a communal reflection by priests and pastoral workers on themes that emerged in the survey. Together we decided that three areas of concern seemed most urgent: (1) the shift in images of ministry and in expectations among pastoral staff; (2) the widely experienced difficulty in dealing with the conflicts that arise as closer working relationships develop; and (3) the need for shared understandings of different styles of cooperation in ministry.

The planning group also decided that the communal process should explicitly examine the Christian tradition and cultural influences on these three questions.

The planning group was committed to a conference format that modeled collaboration. To that end, a two and one-half day conference was designed, beginning with a communal reflection on the current state of shared ministry in their diocese and concluding with a communal evaluation of the conference days and an effort to enunciate next steps in this new style of ministry.

3. The Process Begins: Listening to Experience

Two hundred and fifty participants were in attendance: more than a hundred lay persons in various service roles joined the diocese's two bishops, approximately seventy priests, and seventy religious sisters and brothers. Results of the survey instrument had been distributed to all participants prior to the assembly, to serve as background information for the sessions. At the conference, members of the local planning team itself guided the initial process, asking each table of eight persons to consider two questions: "What do we hope to learn about collaborative ministry through this conference" and "What positive developments in collaborative ministry are taking place through the diocese today?"

After some table discussion, a representative of each discussion group reported its chief convictions. These convictions were recorded on large newsprint sheets and posted on the wall of the assembly room for everyone to read.

The most common responses to the first question were requests for a clearer definition of collaborative ministry, a desire to see examples in the diocese where shared ministry was actually in place, a hope to learn more about how to deal with conflicts that inevitably arise among close colleagues. One response in particular stirred the group: "What are the conversions we face in trying to work together this way?"

Responses to the second question ranged from praise for a collaborative planning project currently underway in the diocese, to gratitude for religious congregations of women who have modeled new styles of shared leadership, to a recognition of a more receptive and listening mood among the official leaders in the diocese. In a more adversarial tone, members of one table discussion suggested that asking for only positive developments was manipulative.

Throughout the morning, the energy among the participants was high; the group seemed to relish this experience of a broad section of the diocese together at work.

The Changing Shape of Ministry

Our contribution in the conference itself began in the afternoon, with a brief reflection on the profound changes in ministry in the past three decades. Thirty years ago, a gathering of diocesan pastoral leaders such as this would have included only priests and bishops. Today a range of Christians—women and men, lay persons as well as religious and clergy—gather to explore their shared vocations of service to the church and world. Enthusiasm for collaboration surged in the 1970s, as Catholics rejoiced in new opportunities to share the life of faith. Convinced that joint action would accomplish more than individual effort, many in ministry sought out colleagues. But over the past decade, this initial enthusiasm for shared ministry has mellowed. Many recognize now how difficult this effort is! Differing visions of the church, of authority, of the place of anger and conflict in our shared life—all these differences make for ongoing disagreements and frequently defeat efforts to work together. Sobered by the difficulty of becoming genuine colleagues in ministry, experienced pastoral workers acknowledge that the challenges ahead involve more than skill or technique. The Christian body is being called to a radical conversion: to see *women*, and *leaders*, and *laity* in a new light; to re-imagine Christian ministry itself.

1. The Tradition Changes: From Parents to Partners

Christians have traditionally used the images and vocabulary of family to describe the church. Holy Mother Church thrived under the leadership of our Holy Father; the leader of a congregation of women religious was often called "mother superior," and the pastor in the parish is still called "father." In this world-wide family, we are all the children of God. And when church is understood as family, seeing leaders in the role of parents seems natural.

In the profound transformations begun in the Second Vatican Council, the Catholic church moved toward the vision of itself as an adult community. As adults experience themselves called to serve others in response to the gospel, they aspire to minister as *partners* of traditional leaders rather than as their child-like assistants. Vatican II evoked ancient memories in the Body of Christ: the recollection of Jesus telling his disciples to "call no one your father on earth, for you have one Father—the one in heaven," (Matthew 23) and reminding us that we are all sisters and brothers of one another; memories of St. Paul's conviction (Galatians 3) that in Baptism the once-essential distinctions between free and slave, Greek and Jew, male and female lose their traditional force, opening the community to the hopes and demands of real mutuality. These disquieting memories from our religious heritage suggest a new style of religious leadership, characterized more by partnership than parenting. At this point in the discussion several participants noted a parallel shift in the business world: a hierarchical style of leadership is being replaced by "quality circles" and a partnering style of decision making. As the community of faith responds to these changes in both tradition and culture, our inherited images of life together and our inherited structures of leadership come under review.

2. Reflecting on Experience

Participants were then asked to reflect on their own experience of these alternate visions of the role of the religious leader: *parenting* and *partnership*. The following exercise was used.

Recall your life and service within the community of faith these days: in the parish, as member of a prayer group or ministry team, working in a religious office or agency. Take time to be present to the range of your participation in church life.

Drawing on this personal experience, identify a recent incident in church life in which the understanding of *ministry as parenting* prevailed. Spend some time with the experience itself: What was the setting? Who was involved? What was the outcome?

As you look back on this incident, what do you see as the strengths or benefits of this style of ministry? What, for you, are its limitations?

Then identify a recent incident in which the understanding of *ministry as partnership* was in evidence. Again, spend time with the experience: the setting, the people involved, the outcome.

From your perspective, what were the benefits or strengths of this style of ministry? What were its limitations?

The table discussion that followed generated many examples of each style, along with candid evaluations of the strengths and limits of each. Parenting styles of religious leadership and ministry were acknowledged to serve well, for example, when working with children and young people, in a variety of pastoral counseling settings, at early stages of some group projects. Limitations to this style that were noted included a tendency toward authoritarian behavior, lack of mutual accountability, loss of access to the full range of resources in the group, and alienation of many potential colleagues.

Partnership styles of ministry and leadership were seen as valuable in most small group settings (pastoral staff, working groups, diocesan committees, small faith communities). Many respondents noted the importance of partnership styles in settings where questions of corporate mission and goals were under discussion and debate. Benefits identified in the partnership style included an enhanced sense of commitment, broader participation, better outcomes, expansion of the group's resources. Comments on the limitations of the partnership style concentrated on the increased demands experienced by both leaders and others: more time seems to be required to clarify expectations and come to decisions; lines of accountability sometimes remain unclear, leading to problems later; most of us are still new in the practice of partnership and, therefore, not always consistent in our behavior or attitudes.

When the group returned from table discussion to the large assembly, several respondents affirmed the benefits of both parenting and partnership: both contribute to a vital ministry, but the stances are very different. Others noted that many institutional structures enshrine and defend ministry as parenting; most of our images of obedience and conflict are rooted in a sense of our common life as familial—a few parents and many children. A common refrain was the disparity between the gospel vision of mutuality and equality in faith, and ecclesial structures and practice which still endorse an inequality of women and all lay persons. Planners were relieved that this mood of candid lament did not degenerate into accusations of blame. Rather, the group acknowledged the difficulties that stand in the way of its own aspirations for a more effective experience of ministering together. This public acknowledgement helped the group set its own goals for growth and conversion.

Listening to Tradition on Conflict

The discussion of different visions of ministry and leadership led directly into the question of conflict—the second concern that had surfaced in the survey as troublesome for many in the diocese. As we become partners in ministry, how are we to manage the unavoidable and painful embrace of conflict?

This stage of the diocesan reflection began with a session on the morning of the second day, focusing on this difficult dynamic in our lives of shared faith. The management of conflict begins in clarifying assumptions about who we are and how we are together. If we see ourselves simply as docile children of authoritative parents, disagreement and dissent have no place. For a long time in our religious tradition conflict has been stigmatized as disobedience and infidelity. If our leaders know what is best for us, what right have we to question their judgments? An adult church in which all the baptized are called to active participation must learn how to embrace in conflict without injuring one another, how to disagree with charity and confront with civility. Returning to Scripture helps Christians recognize conflict as an essential element of ecclesial life.

In Galatians 2, Paul recounts his disagreement with Peter and James over a crucial issue of ministry—whether to circumcise new converts who were not Jews. Peter and James are authoritative "pillars of the church," disciples of Jesus from the start. Paul is a "late arrival," neither an original apostle nor companion of Jesus in his lifetime. Yet Paul, disagreeing with these authorities, argues his case with energy and persistence. Heated debate ensued; the very identity of the movement seemed at stake. Finally the participants reached a compromise that resolved the conflict. Then, in Paul's report, Peter and James extend their hand "in partnership" (*koinonia*). This hand shake seals a partnership in ministry that has survived the threat of conflict.

Not always celebrated in this story is a special lesson about conflict. Often it is in conflict, even by means of conflict, that the future is revealed. This early conflict among the first generation of Jesus' followers was both painful and generative. Their disagreement brought deeper understanding. In this struggle, a broader vision of the church emerged. This insight from our religious heritage is reinforced by contemporary observers of cultural change. Philosopher John Anderson reiterates the importance of disagreement: "It is through conflict, and sometimes only through conflict that we learn what our ends and purposes are."[4]

A Return to Experience

Participants were asked to recall, in a moment of prayerful recollection, a recent experience of conflict. The instructions were: Remember a work relationship, in your pastoral life or elsewhere, that has been significant for you. Identify some of the disagreements and disputes that have been part of this enduring relationship.

From this list, select a particular conflict that turned out to be fruitful. Spend some time reflecting on the contribution that this distressing experience made—to the quality of the work, to the maturing of the relationship itself.

After some time considering this interpersonal experience of conflict, participants were asked this next question.

Is there a religious institution or organization that you currently hold in conflict? Perhaps your pastoral work site or the parish community; perhaps diocesan leadership or the Vatican bureaucracy. In the midst of this institutional struggle, what is the grace for which you hope?

Sharing experiences at the tables and then in the whole assembly, participants deepened their awareness of how prevalent is conflict in current pastoral experience and how widespread is the personal discomfort it generates. Yet almost all were ready to testify to the valuable contribution that facing conflict had brought into their pastoral relationships. "The process of sharing these stories takes some of the scandal and shame out of conflict," noted one respondent. "Publicly acknowledging that conflict is 'normal,' even among people of good will, makes this a topic we are now able to discuss more honestly," added participants at another table. In the evaluation session that brought the conference to an end on the next day, this public discussion of conflict was cited as a significant advance in openness and honesty among diocesan personnel.

What Does Collaboration Demand? — Consulting Cultural Resources

On the afternoon of the second day, the diocesan reflection turned to the third issue that the survey had surfaced as a major concern: the need for greater clarity and confidence about the goal of partnership in ministry. Once again, the session began with a brief presentation—now relying on cultural resources to offer a model of three organizational styles of working together.

To collaborate is to "labor together," to work together toward a common goal. No one style of "laboring together" suits every pastoral setting. In fact, several organizational patterns can support greater collaboration. We may work together as a *staff*, or as a *team*, or as a *community*: each image offers differing ways to conceptualize how collaborative groups function. Of course, actual groups are always more complex than the model suggests. In practice, many successful pastoral groups incorporate elements from all three organizational patterns. In addition, the model is not a prescription for how pastoral collaboration *should* proceed. It serves best as a guide for discussion, helping pastoral colleagues evaluate their current style to see what needs to be reinforced and what needs to be renegotiated. After a brief presentation of each organizational style, participants were given opportunity to evaluate their current pastoral setting.

1. Staff

A staff is a work group organized into different levels of responsibility. The person in charge holds a higher position than others on the staff. The chain of command moves vertically: directives come down from levels above; staff members are accountable to "higher ups." Co-workers may share information and coordinate schedules, but they usually work alone. The leader's role is highly visible, pictured at the top of a pyramid or at the hub of a wheel. This official leader—understood as manager, supervisor, boss—directs the activities of other staff members.

Functioning as a staff brings clear advantages to an organization with broad outreach and a wide range of programs. The manager/staff design is orderly and efficient. Job descriptions state what each worker's duties are and how much authority each has; established policies announce ahead of time what behavior is expected; clear procedures help staff members act with confidence.

But operating as a staff carries some risks for collaboration. The first is isolation. Staff procedures typically do more to separate co-workers than to bring them together. Official lines of communication move to and from the person in charge. This group leader, as manager, tends to deal with staff members individually. Sometimes this separation serves the work, keeping people out of one another's way and focused on their own responsibilities. But collaboration depends on connections. A staff that wants to work collaboratively has to overcome this built-in separateness. Since the leader plays such a central role in a staff, it is often up to the leader to invite staff members to broaden their collaboration. The leader can set up opportunities for cooperation; the leader can encourage staff members to rely on each others more often.

A second risk to collaboration comes from the pull of formal procedures. Functioning as a staff means working within established roles and rules. Collaboration demands that staff members contribute to keeping these structures flexible. But some organizations resist giving staff members such discretion. When structure becomes master rather than servant, collaboration suffers.

The Experience of Working as a Staff

After presenting these characteristics of a staff, we invited the participants to examine their own efforts of collaboration, using these three cue questions:

- In what ways does our pastoral group operate as a staff?
- How does operating as a staff help us in our ministry?
- How does operating this way make our ministry difficult?

2. Working as a Team

A team is a work group organized for interdependence. On a team people come together more intentionally. If a staff is organized to keep its members out of each others' way, a team intends to have its members get in each other's way. Members of a team have less sharply divided roles. Team members are more available to help each other, not just in emergencies, but by design.

Team members benefit from this access to one another's strengths. Working together expands the group's scope, because it is not limited to what individuals can do on their own. Team members make their experience and skills available to one another; that is part of the promise of team ministry. Functioning as a team, each members has a *right* to others' resources. Members of teams often share the conviction that working closely together is more effective and enjoyable than the efficient but segmented assignments of a staff. A team is often more flexible than a staff. Because it is less likely to be a fully integrated element in an institutional arrangement, the team may be more comfortable with change and more responsive to crises.

The strengths of a team are often offset by certain risks. Within a larger organization such as a diocese or school system, a tight knit team may generate suspicion. By intent, the team does not play by the rules of the larger group. Leadership roles often remain less clearly defined. Institutional administrators may wonder: "What are they up to? Who is *really* in charge? Who do we hold accountable when something goes wrong?"

A challenge for many groups who understand themselves as a team is to *befriend* structure. Sometimes those who gravitate toward teams have been disillusioned in the past by inflexible or authoritarian organizational patterns. This leaves them skeptical of all formal arrangements. But operating without policies and procedures seldom serves collaboration. By putting some rules and roles into place, a team rescues energy for its more important work.

The Experience of Working as a Team

Here, again, participants evaluated their current pastoral setting, using these questions:

- Are there ways our ministry group operates as a team?

- How does acting as a team help us in our ministry?

- How does acting as a team make our ministry difficult?

3. Community

People in pastoral work today often describe themselves as a ministering community. A ministering community is a group in which *shared values* lead to *common action* undertaken in a spirit of *mutual concern*. In a community, members try to balance the agenda of mutual care with the agenda of the pastoral task. They wish to *be something* together as well as *do something* together. Shared values, joint action, and mutual concern are not absent from other pastoral settings. But in a community each of these elements demands *explicit* attention.

Much of the energy behind the movement of groups to become a ministering community lies in their vision of ministry. Ministry is seen as a gift and challenge for the community itself, rather than the calling of individuals. A group gathered as a ministering community wants to witness to this common calling: their life together, with its public visibility, becomes an essential part of its ministry. The ministry of L'Arche groups, for example, offers an instance of this fusion of community and service.

A ministering community is challenged simultaneously on several fronts: to nurture a common vision, to show their concern for one another in genuinely appropriate ways, to act together effectively. Community groups take seriously both their tasks and the quality of their life together. Time demands can be considerable. Activities that help in one area of communal concern may cause problems in another: commitment to proceed by consensus delays an important decision; a regular schedule of communal prayer strengthens group cohesion but draws the complaint that it diverts members from their pastoral work. Ministry groups that become successful communities learn how to live with these tensions, balancing commitment to one another with shared responsibility for the pastoral task.

The Experience of Working as a Ministering Community

Participants once more explored their own pastoral setting, using these questions:

- Concretely, in what ways does our ministry group operate as a community?

- How does our functioning as a community help us in ministry?

- How does functioning as a community make our ministry more difficult?

Then, based on the model as a whole, a final evaluation task was posed: From this analysis of your own pastoral setting, please comment on:

- one element of our current operating style that helps this pastoral group act at its best . . .

- one element of our current operating style that needs modification now . . .

Pastoral Response

The final morning of the conference began with a rich liturgical moment: participants, each with a lit candle, processed into the darkened assembly room; in prayers and hymns the group revisited the themes and sharings of the past two days.

After this prayerful beginning, participants were asked to respond to two questions: (1) What have I gotten out of the past two days? (2) What am I ready to commit myself to do, in order to strengthen partnership in ministry in our diocese?

First in small table gatherings and then before the entire assembly, people spoke of the honesty and richness of the sharing over the past days. They appreciated coming to greater clarity about the different forms that collaboration can take, recognizing that no automatic "right answer" exists for every group. One table group urged a set of common "definition of terms" be developed in the diocese, to help the discussion about collaboration proceed. Another group suggested that the reflective exercises used in the conference be distributed to every parish, with encouragement that local groups use these tools to stimulate peer conversation.

Several individuals spoke of committing themselves to be more open to face the necessary conflicts in their pastoral settings. Some expressed their regret that current leaders in some parishes resisted sharing power, making genuine collaboration an unlikely goal. Representatives of other parishes regretted the absence of colleagueship in their own work, due to a lack of finances necessary to support expanded staff. These persons challenged the diocese to find more creative ways to distribute its resources, both financial and personnel. For example, could more wealthy parishes support a youth minister or religious education teacher in a poorer parish?

The planning committee, too, had been involved in this final reflection exercise and made its own report to the participant assembly. These members saluted the enthusiasm and commitment evident throughout the conference itself and re-committed themselves to their mandate to advance collaborative ministry in the diocese. The committee announced three steps to be taken, with a timeline for each. First, within one month a record of the table responses and personal evaluation statements would be compiled and distributed to all conference participants. Members of the diocesan pastoral council would receive a summary of this material.

Second, in response to the energetic discussion that followed the conflict presentation, the staff of a local retreat house had volunteered to develop and offer a course to train local parishioners and pastoral ministers in skills of conflict identification and negotiation. The planning team committed to working closely with the retreat house to determine the feasibility of such a program; a decision was promised within six months.

Third, a wider "follow-up team" would be established, including one representative from each of the seven deaneries of the diocese as well as the current planning group. Its goal is to prepare a practical agenda for the diocese on "where do we go from here" over the next three years in implementing greater collaboration in ministry. The response of this conference's participants will be core information from which the agenda is developed, so members of the follow-up team will be selected from participants. This action agenda will be formally presented to the diocesan pastoral council within nine months.

As the conference discussion came to a close, several respondents thanked the two bishops for their active participation in the conference and their continuing support for efforts of pastoral collaboration. A Eucharistic celebration brought the assembly to a close.

Notes

1. Jack Shea, "Doing Ministerial Theology," in D. Tracy, ed., *Toward Vatican III* (New York: Seabury, 1978), p. 188.

2. See Mary Benet McKinney, *Sharing Wisdom: A Process for Group Decision Making* (Allen, TX: Tabor Publishing, 1987) and Kennon L. Callahan, *Effective Church Leadership* (HarperSanFrancisco, 1990). The Chicago-based Parish Evaluation Project (2200 E. Devon; Des Plaines, IL 60018) has developed a range of eminently practical research instruments for effective pastoral planning. See Thomas Sweetser and Carol Wisniewski Holden, *Leadership in a Successful Parish* (Kansas City: Sheed & Ward, 1990) and Thomas Sweetser and Patricia Forster, *Transforming the Parish* (Kansas City: Sheed & Ward, 1993). The Alban Institute (4550 Montgomery Avenue; Bethesda, MD 20814) provides publications and training programs to strengthen effective pastoral response; see the Institute's monthly publication, *Congregations*.

3. The observations on collaboration and conflict that we offered in this conference are developed further in our *Promise of Partnership: A Model for Collaborative Ministry* (HarperSanFrancisco, 1993).

4. Alisdair MacIntyre quotes Anderson in *After Virtue* (Notre Dame, IN: University of Notre Dame Press, 1981), p. 152.

• Part Four •

Pastoral Reflection at Work

The enthusiasm for theological reflection in the community of faith grows as Christians claim communal discernment as part of their religious call. In the chapters that follow, several colleagues share their own work in support of such pastoral reflection. Patricia O'Connell Killen describes ways that pastors and other religious educators can assist adults to reflect theologically on their lives. Peter Buttitta presents a style of reflection he has developed to support new ministries emerging in the context of health care. Ada María Isasi-Díaz outlines a method she employs to draw out and validate the life experience of Hispanic women as a source of theological reflection. Robert Schreiter reflects on the challenge of reconciliation among Catholic Christians in the unique cultural context of contemporary China. These examples of pastoral reflection, each with a particular focus and a distinctive approach, display the vitality of the conversation that is theological reflection in ministry today.

· 8 ·

Assisting Adults to Think Theologically

Patricia O'Connell Killen

THERE IS NO TASK MORE CRUCIAL FOR ANYONE WORKING WITH ADULTS IN the church today than helping them to think theologically. Without this skill, Christians lack the conscious and critical access to the resources of their tradition that both the church and the world desperately need.

Without theological reflection on the part of adult Christians, the church's faithfulness to the gospel and its authentic witness diminishes. Why? Because our capacity to comprehend and faithfully live the Christian faith correlates directly with our capacity to discover the revelatory quality of our human experience. And our capacity to live rich, authentic human lives depends on our ability to enter deeply and openly into our Christian heritage. Tapping the inherently dynamic and energy-filled connection between our lives and the Christian heritage is the core of theological reflection.[1]

Theological knowledge, like all wisdom, is both liberating and dangerous. Developmentally, many adults initially approach the tradition presuming there is an authority here that is always correct and holds clear answers to life's demands. When adults respond to an invitation to begin theological reflection, then, they often do so believing theology to be a set of general rules which they can apply to their lives. Their hope is to learn these rules and their application so their lives will be better.

The invitation to think theologically calls people to relate to their religious heritage in a new way. They begin to notice and care about their own and others' lives. They understand that truth has contexts, that knower and known are intimately connected. Now the tradition is understood as the collective wisdom of the past and present community. The tradition carries particular weight as trustworthy, but it is not the single absolute in someone's life.[2] As with most good conversation partners, the tradition begins to provide both delightful and discomforting surprises, opening new angles of vision on our lives.

Engaging in theological reflection shows people that the tradition is dynamic and growing. They recognize that they are carriers and shapers of the tradition, just as it has carried and formed them. They grasp—cognitively and affectively—that to be faithful means adapting tradition in new settings. And faithfulness also demands an appropriation of the tradition which allows it to ground potential critique of new circumstances, attitudes and actions which run counter to our best understandings of the gospel.[3] The tradition carries us and we carry it; in the process we are mutually sustained and transformed.

Creating the Context

The best context for assisting adults to think theologically is a group which meets regularly for theological reflection over an extended period of time. Regular practice and learning from that practice—doing theological reflection and then looking at what was done—is crucial if theological thinking is to become a conscious and critical part of the lives of Christian adults today.[4]

Given that theological thinking is, at its best, a corporate endeavor, the rules which apply for effective groups in other settings apply here. Basic people skills are essential. Adults must learn to say "I," to speak what they mean, to listen, to clarify, to engage in conflict openly. These adult communication skills are crucial for open and genuine theological conversation.

Because the group is a small community of faithful engaging their Christian heritage, two other elements for the context are crucial. First, regular prayer should be included. Corporate prayer nurtures and supports openness, trust, and courage in individuals as they grow in relation to each other and to God's action. Such prayer creates space for significant insights and growth to occur as a result of theological thinking. Second, assisting theological thinking is most easily done when the members of the group are studying the tradition in some way, whether that study be Scripture, church history, or theology. Without study, the theological thinking which goes on in the group cannot deepen beyond the level of knowledge in the group at its starting point. The tradition is richer and bigger than any adult knows. Disciplined study is part of taking one's tradition seriously.[5]

Finally, for the leader, the one who will assist adults to think theologically: Do not undertake the task unless you are willing to commit quality presence, careful preparation, and a willingness to improve your own theological skills to the group, for six-to-nine months or longer. The habit of theological thinking takes time and practice to learn. Assisting adults to think theologically is neither a quick fix nor low investment educational program.[6]

Theological Reflection and Meaning-Making

Adults learn theological thinking best when it is connected to processes which they already know. Indeed, the human quality of theological thinking is a crucial fact to get across to adults who want to do theology. So, before focusing directly on such thinking, set theological reflection in the context of human beings' innate activity of making meaning. Born biologically unfinished, without the instinctual capacities that would allow us, like puppies, to know to get in out of the rain, we come to be human in interaction with our families and larger culture, all the time learning to make sense of our experience with the resources which they provide us. By the time we come to self-consciousness, we have already absorbed a meaning-making or interpretive framework from our culture. Our relationship to that framework changes and grows as we develop, depending on the degree of our self-consciousness and on the kinds of experiences we have.[7]

While much of our life goes by with events, ideas, and emotions easily fitting into our comfortable meaning-making framework, all of us pause to reflect sooner or later. We reflect when something happens to us that cannot readily fit into our current interpretive frameworks: a question—Why did you do that?, a disturbance—the serious rift in a longterm friendship, an experience of beauty—hearing a poem or the embrace of a child. Whatever the experience, it refuses to settle into one's regular meaning-making framework and so will not go away. It remains present in one's memory and body.

Reflection is the act of deliberately slowing down our habitual meaning-making processes to take a closer look at the experience and at our meaning-making framework. This takes courage because it makes us vulnerable in two ways: (1) we reexperience the event, including the feelings that were there, and (2) we open our meaning-making or interpretive framework to revision; all our most dearly held beliefs, biases, convictions, and ways of responding to life may be called into question.[8]

Theology and Theological Reflection

As content or information—what a religious tradition teaches about the divine, the human, the created order, and their interrelationships—theology is the fruit of a reflective process. Theological content is not a timeless, ahistorical body of information couched in language that can be understood readily in any time or place. Theological reflection is a process of making meaning of selves and the world in light of God, carried on by persons with particular questions arising from particular experiences in particular cultural situations who are members of particular communities of faith. Each generation and community must translate its experience for the tradition and the tradition for its life, if its theology is to be life-giving and faithful.[9]

Steps in Theological Thinking

While the theologies we read and hear can seem confusing and diverse, there are fundamental elements in the process of theological thinking common to all of them. In assisting adults to think theologically, begin with these common basic dynamics: the nonjudgmental narration of experience, identifying the heart of the matter, structuring a correlation between contemporary experience and the tradition, and identifying new learnings and calls to action for our lives. While these will look different depending on the length, purpose, and scope of the theological reflection that is done, they are common to what happens in an adult theological reflection group in a parish and what happens when a theologian writes a book.[10]

1. Nonjudgmental Narration of Experience

If we want to assist adults to enter into such a dynamic, mutual conversation between their experience and their religious heritage, a basic skill to teach them is the nonjudgmental narration of experience. Without this, the entire theological process is short-circuited.

By experience, I mean what we have done and what has happened to us as we have interacted with our environments: with our self, family, natural world, religious heritage, and wider culture.[11]

Narrating experience in a nonjudgmental manner is not easy, because such narration takes us back to the event. It makes the incident present again as we re-experience the feelings and action, see the scene, smell the smells, sense the impressions.

Being present again is a vulnerable spot. But it is also the place where God is. The event is where God was at that time. There is revelation in an event which remains with us. The events that remain in our memories and bodies are the ones for which we have not yet fully grasped nor fully lived the meaning. Our lived experiences are the only events with which we can weave the ongoing tapestry of our lives.

Nonjudgmental narration involves giving the "who," "what," "when," "where," and "how" of an event. A narration is concrete, it hooks the five senses and involves the entire person. Those who listen to a nonjudgmental narration find themselves able to be present with the teller in the situation.

What a narration does not include is "why." The answer to "why" is an interpretation. Genuine interpretation gives us a meaningful "why" to an event, an explanation or account that fits and satisfies. But we bring an event to reflection precisely because our current interpretation of it is inadequate.

When an event does not fit our meaning-making frameworks, we find ourselves retelling it over and over, filled with "shoulds," "should nots," "oughts," "musts," "wish I had," and "if only," to name a few. These are all clues to inadequate meaning-making. They reveal that the experience does not fit into our framework. Still, we keep trying to stuff it in anyway. Disciplined reflection can happen only when we stop stuffing and become present again to the experience.[12]

The same rule of nonjudgmental narration applies when the reflection begins with a piece of the tradition or a current event. My accent on nonjudgmental narration is aimed at getting adults to slow down their meaning-making process in order to be able to look at the event and at their interpretive frameworks. Adults must learn to distinguish between the situation or text and their assumptions, biases, and judgments, regarding it. Their assumptions and biases are legitimate parts of the conversation, but only when clearly identified and owned for what they are.

Another way to approach nonjudgmental narration of experience, especially when focusing on a scriptural text, doctrine, or incident from church history, is to think in terms of defamiliarizing the text.[13] Learning to do historical-critical or literary readings of the tradition occasions this defamiliarization process.[14] The crucial point is for adults to hear the text with fresh ears, to receive the surprises it contains, to recognize heretofore unnoticed nuances and perspectives. Without defamiliarizing the text of tradition, adults will not read it; rather, they will read onto it their preconceived positions.

2. Identifying the Heart of the Matter

Whether one begins theological reflection with adults from their experience, from a social situation, or from a piece of the tradition, another basic skill for theological thinking is identifying the heart of the matter. The heart of the matter is the issue, question, or wonderment that the starting incident or text for reflection carries. What was said earlier about nonjudgmental narration of experience and defamiliarizing the text applies here. Help adults to articulate the heart of the matter in a way which is gentle, reverent, and accurate. Most incidents and texts contain many possible issues and topics. The artful practice here is for adults to learn to sense the issue or question that contains the most energy at the time of reflection. Other issues will not be lost; if significant, they will return at another time.

A range of ways exist to articulate the heart of the matter, from drawing or sculpting an image to writing out a question, to providing a detailed social analysis of a situation. However articulated, the statement of the heart of the matter needs to carry the living energy of the presenting incident, situation, or text and provide some cognitive distance so that reflective analysis can be done.[15]

3. Structuring a Correlation

Correlation is the technical theological term for structuring a conversation between the heart of the matter in our experience and a piece of the Christian tradition. By tradition, I mean the entire lore of Christianity—Scripture, church history, doctrine, theology, lives of the saints, popular devotions, etc.[16]

The correlation provides the context for a real conversation between our lived experience and the tradition. It makes room for the surprise and challenge occasioned by new insights and for the deepened understandings and appreciations of things already known which theological thinking often brings.

Structuring an engaging correlation is crucial to assisting adults to think theologically. The fundamental strategy for structuring a correlation is to form a single question that you use to probe the material brought to the reflection from current experience and from the tradition. Knowing what question to ask and how to shape it requires practice. Learning to listen for the theological themes about which people talk in their ordinary language is one step in developing such a skill.

Christian doctrines or themes provide a fundamental resource for finding questions for structuring correlations. Christian doctrines are answers to basic and, perhaps, universal human questions. Most Christians have learned the answers separate from the context of their originating questions. As a result, doctrine for them is at best irrelevant and mute and at worst oppressive and threatening. To structure a genuine conversation between our experience and the tradition requires that we engage the tradition's wisdom prior to the level of formulaic answers and do so out of our own existential issues.

The skill one must learn to facilitate adults' theological reflection: Identify the questions to which classic Christian themes are the answers. Be able to ask those questions without using theological code language. Put the question to which the doctrine is a response in the language of current human living.[17]

4. Identifying New Learnings and Calls to Action

If theological thinking is to be more than a passing pleasurable intellectual exercise, participants must lay hold of a significant new or deepened insight, or accept the call to new action in their lives. Theological thinking creates an engaging, challenging, and often playful space. Many ideas and insights come during a reflection. No one can remember and act on all of them. But the idea or insight that might be most significant is likely to be forgotten upon leaving, precisely because it alters one's habitual meaning-making interpretive frameworks. So, if people are going to claim something from a theological reflection, they must do so actively, by writing it down, embodying it in clay or words or dance. They may also want to invite support from group members to take a specific action as a first step in living by the new insight. It was nothing for Paul to get knocked off his horse on the road to Damascus. It took a lifetime to live out the implications of that encounter with the risen Christ. Why should we expect our faith journeys to be any different?[18]

Conclusion

These, then, are the fundamental steps in any process of theological reflection: nonjudgmental narration of experience (understood broadly as any source for reflection, e.g., personal experience, social situation, scriptural text); identification of the heart of the matter; putting the heart of the matter into conversation with the wisdom of our Christian heritage; and identifying new insights and actions to which our reflection calls us.

Learning to move through these steps in a conscious and critical manner takes time and practice. It is well worth the effort. When adults begin to relate to their Christian heritage with the same level of intellectual sophistication with which they relate to the rest of their personal and professional lives, they are better able to embody the gospel in our world and are open to receive the richness which their Christian heritage offers them.

As well, such adults begin to understand how their theological reflection process relates to the larger theological conversation carried on by professional theologians and church leaders. They begin to ask questions about the sources which bishops and theologians use and about how they use them in writing on a religious issue. They begin to understand that the professional theologian engages in a more complex, lengthy, and nuanced process of identifying the heart of the matter in a situation, putting it into conversation with the wisdom of the Christian religious heritage, and identifying the resulting truth and insights which can guide people toward richer understandings and experiences of their tradition. At this point, adults have become intelligent partners in the theological conversation. Their growing access to and understanding of the theological heritage allows them to take their rightful place in the work of evangelization and ministry as we enter the twenty-first century.

Notes

1. Patricia O'Connell Killen and John de Beer, *The Art of Theological Reflection* (New York: Crossroad, 1994), Introduction and Chapter 1.

2. Mary Belenky, Mary Field, Blythe McVicker Clinchy, Nancy Rule Goldberger, and Jill Mattuck Tarule, *Women's Ways of Knowing: The Development of Self, Voice, and Mind* (New York: Basic Books, 1986, pp. 131-52.

3. David Tracy, *The Analogical Imagination: Christian Theology and the Culture of Pluralism* (New York: Crossroad, 1981), pp. 99-102.

4. The Institute of Pastoral Studies at Loyola University in Chicago offers workshops and consultation on adult theological reflection programs.

5. Patricia O'Connell Killen and John de Beer, "Everyday Theology: A Model for Religious and Theological Education," *Chicago Studies* (August 1983), pp. 191-206.

6. *Art of Theological Reflection*, pp. 111-16.

7. See Jack Shea, *Stories of God: An Unauthorized Biography* (Chicago: Thomas More Press, 1978), pp. 11-75 and Peter Berger, *The Sacred Canopy* (New York: Doubleday Anchor, 1969), pp. 3-28.

8. *Art of Theological Reflection*, pp. x-xi; Shea, *Stories of God*, pp. 11-15.

9. Tracy, *Analogical Imagination*, p. 99.

10. On differences in terms of length, scope, and purpose of theology, see the Whiteheads' discussion in the Introduction to this volume and James Hug, *Tracing the Spirit: Communities, Social Action, and Theological Reflection* (New York: Paulist Press, 1983), pp. 2-4.

11. Shea, *Stories of God*, pp. 15-18.

12. *Art of Theological Reflection*, pp. 20-27.

13. I am indebted to my colleague, Jack Shea, for this concept.

14. See, for example, Jack Shea's approach in *The Spirit Master* (Chicago: Thomas More Press, 1987).

15. *Art of Theological Reflection*, pp. 63-66; 122-27.

16. See "Everyday Theology: A Model for Religious and Theological Education," p. 193 and *Art of Theological Reflection*, pp. 53-61.

17. *Art of Theological Reflection*, pp. 127-39.

18. *Art of Theological Reflection*, pp. 66-68; 139-141.

• 9 •

Theological Reflection in Health Ministry: A Strategy for Parish Nurses

Peter K. Buttitta

GOD IS FAITHFULLY PRESENT TO THE CIRCUMSTANCES OF OUR LIVES. AMID the diverse collection of thoughts, urges, beliefs, emotions and memories which make up our interior life, God acts to deepen our awareness and inform our decisions in the direction of the good, the just, the holy. Theological reflection is a way of intentionally looking beneath the surface of our daily activities to discover the presence of God there. It is a way of noticing the *more* that exists within ourselves, in others and within our day-to-day interactions.

Over the past decade I have been involved, in both hospital and parish settings, in developing the Parish Nurse Ministry. While nurses have been able to adapt their professional skills to the parish setting readily, many have expressed a desire to sharpen their pastoral skills and deepen their faith life, their spirituality. Working closely with a group of parish nurses, I developed a pastoral resource to respond to that request.

The purpose in developing this reflective strategy is threefold. First, it is meant to help health ministers befriend theology. Theology's terminology is alien and uninviting to many outside the discipline. The pastoral tool serves to remind nurses that they, too, are involved in reflecting on God's presence and action.

Second, the resource encourages reflection on one's own work. Ours is a society that tends not to value or encourage reflection. North Americans are geared toward action, motion, sound and stimulation. In our ministry, though, we sometimes need to be still. To remain in health care ministry we must continue to deepen our awareness of God's presence with it. We must recognize that "in giving we receive" not just by feeling good about our work but because we are changed in the process.

The third reason for developing this resource is to help the church benefit from the experience generated in this new ministry. Just as we believe that God was present within the scandalous torture and execution of Jesus, calling him through death to life, so we trust that God is present in all the events of our own lives, calling us into new ways of being. By reflecting on their health ministry experiences and naming the issues and graces they find there, parish nurses minister to the church's need to understand more deeply its call.

Starting in Experience

We begin with our stories, stories of triumph, stories of failure. Theological reflection honors our stories, accepting them as valid and meaningful, even if not always whole. By starting with our stories, pastoral reflection helps us sit with brokenness, offering hope without trivializing or ignoring the reality of suffering. It can do this because, by using our experience as a starting point, we are not as likely to try and force our experience to fit into a predetermined theological category. We are more open, instead, to submit ourselves to the transforming presence of God within the situation.

The language of theology helps us name our experiences of God. Therefore, pastoral reflection looks for connections between our lived faith and our religious tradition. Exploring our experience and our religious heritage is expanded when we include cultural information in the conversation. Culture is the collection of symbols, mores, and sciences in our society. It includes language and role definitions, as well as the influence of our family systems and that of the people with whom we minister. Theological reflection considers all three of these areas—personal experience, religious tradition, and culture—to be *sources* of pastorally significant insight. By *attending* to each source individually and then *asserting* them together, we end up with a broader array of theologically significant information upon which to base our *decisions and action.*

For those of us in health ministry, this way of systematically probing our experience can have an important effect on our work. It can help us name the urges that we feel within us, which have called us into this new way of responding in health care. It will challenge our preconceived notions about what parish ministry should look like, of what limits we should put on our work. It can give us validation when we feel diminished; it can help to sustain us when the novelty has worn off and all we have left are seemingly unfulfilled expectations. Besides the effect on personal spirituality and practice, theological reflection will serve the field of health ministry as well. It can help refine and expand the theological premises that have been offered as rationale for our ministry. At the same time, reflection on the work of parish nursing can aid the writing of standards of care and practice by grounding these guidelines in actual cases.

A Strategy for Pastoral Reflection

Now we move step-by-step through a particular process of theological reflection. This method shares several core elements with other pastoral approaches: choosing an experience to reflect upon, describing that experience, examining it, and drawing forth from it insight for future actions. In addition, the method presented here has these specific characteristics:

• It takes into account the fact that health ministry is a comparatively new field. Therefore, there is a need and a desire to examine actual cases in order to determine standards of practice, to test limits and check out assumptions. This method builds the theological reflection into the review of the situation from the point of view of nursing and allied disciplines.

• While it begins in solitude, as you choose one event from your life toward which to attend, it works best as a group exercise. A group is more likely to see the many facets of a particular experience and keeps an individual from distorting or misreading an experience. Also, a group helps keep you committed to the process, month to month, year to year.

• It recognizes that parish nurses rarely have advanced theology degrees, but that their deliberate attention to God's movement within their lives is a characteristic of what it means to be spiritually mature.

• It promotes the use of the imagination, by means of images and metaphors, in order to move beyond our taken-for-granted faith to the level of critical reflection and transformation.

The steps of the method can be worked through by an individual in a half-hour to an hour. The group reflection can be done comfortably in about one hour. Naturally, the more time given, the more connections that can be made and, therefore, the richer the reflection.

The Method

Step 1: *Choose an event to reflect upon.*

Choose an interaction with an individual or a family; in their home or at the parish; or perhaps a staff meeting in which you felt emotionally invested. Even a health educational program or a exercise class can offer a rich reflection.

Choose one from your life that is recent, within the past two weeks or so, toward which you have some energy or some unclarity. Our questions are often the place where God is attempting to break through in a new way.

Do not worry too much about which event to choose. As pastoral theologian Robert Kinast reminds us, "There are no criteria which will guarantee a perfect selection every time. Important experiences often occur subtly, suggesting that something more is going on than just matter-of-fact activities. Important events convey a sense of something larger, more essential to life, more engaging or demanding, thicker with meaning than most events."[1]

Step 2: *Recall the specifics of the event.*

Tell the story: what happened, where were you? What came first, what was the result? Highlight who the main "players" were and how they were related to one another. In other words, start by answering the questions "who, what, when, where, and how." Add as many details as are important to the dynamics of the situation. The point is to reenter the event as closely as possible in order to understand its meaning and message. In sharing it with the group, the details help the others enter the experience with you.

Let's look at an example from the ministry of parish nurse Carey Wilson who works in the inner city:

> I got a call one hot September Monday from Fr. Bob from our neighboring parish. He asked if I would go with him to visit Myra S., a 63-year-old woman who has lived on the streets, but was recently settled in an apartment. He has been visiting her and looking out for her, and wondered if I would be willing to connect with her. I agreed to visit her with him, because it sounded like she was someone who is truly not served by orthodox structures, and also because he said she had some psychiatric problems—one area in which I feel pretty comfortable.
>
> Around 2 p.m. we arrived at a seedy-looking apartment building—one of many on this particular block—and walked up

one flight to her apartment. After a peep at us, and an, "Oh, you're with someone," she shut the door and there was about a five minute wait and some scuffling before she let us in. The apartment was one of my visions of hell: old, dirty blankets and yellowed foam blocks jumbled on a sagging mattress; ashtrays filled to the brim with butts; newspapers, bags, and junk over most of the small floor space; a dirty stove; beer cans lined up precariously on a dresser that listed several inches to one side; flies buzzing in and out of a dusty fan, and roaches meandering through it all.

She invited us to sit down on the two chairs; she sat on the bed. Her first comment to me was, "The color of your hair is so pretty." She, herself, had a beautiful smile and a spark about her I liked. Father Bob asked whether she was eating well. She said she had eaten breakfast, but it seemed unclear how many other meals she had had. He also asked her what her most pressing errand was. She wanted to get rabies shots for her two dogs, which he agreed to do. She also needed to get a public aid card, but he allowed her to make the decision of getting the shots first. I invited her to church, and she said she had already been there. It sounded like she wanted to make even more of a connection there. When we parted, I said I hoped I would see her again, and she seemed open to this.

Notice that Carey, in this initial description of the situation, avoids answering the WHY question. She does not attempt to explain Ms. S's behavior or Fr. Bob's. Instead, she tells the story, which will carry the questions to the next steps.

Besides the Case Study format used here, you can also present the specifics of the event by means of the Verbatim Case Study.[2] You may also want to describe the situation as a nursing case study and include such information as diagnosis, vital signs, medications, lab results, and nursing plan. Again, the point is to reenter the situation in order to understand its meaning and message.

Step 3: *Recall your feelings during this event and any bodily sensations generated by it.*

What were you feeling during this situation? What was happening in your body?

The meaning you assign to this event is related to your feelings toward it, physical and emotional. Feelings carry our questions and point to possible answers. Bodily sensations can be interpreted as "symbolizing" at a basic level the meaning this event has for you. You may notice that there are many sayings in our language which are body-related, such as, "It was a thorn in my side," "What a pain in the neck," "You tickle my funny bone," "I just had a gut feeling." This event is related to you corporally through these sensations; listen to your own "body language."

For example, while reflecting on her case, Carey remembered being worried that either roaches or fleas were going to "attach" themselves to her, which made her *itch*. She also felt a wave of *nausea* from the smell. She felt *revulsion* at the chaos in the apartment and *powerless* to change any of it. A feeling of *relief* came over her as she left the apartment and Fr. Bob took Ms. S. to the animal hospital by himself. Carey also says she at the same time felt *attracted* to Ms. S., and wanted to get to know her better.

Recalling your feelings helps uncover where the energy is for you in this situation, and what it is that draws your attention the most. In naming your feelings, be aware of your attitude *toward* feelings. Are they a problem, are they a resource? For theological reflection, our feelings are a gift, an *incarnation* of our questions before we can name them. You may feel uncomfortable in sharing your feelings, but noticing them realistically is important to this method.

Step 4: *Name the main issue(s) or value(s) at play in this situation, and the cultural factors affecting them.*

What value is being expressed by the words or actions of the main "players"? Are there conflicting values being expressed? What issues are at play?

The main issue for Carey was how involved to get with Ms. S. Carey's first impulse was to "clean up" Ms. S.'s life—literally, to clean her apartment, take her to the soup kitchen, give her some food from the food pantry, take her to a doctor, help her get her public aid card, and help her get shots for her dogs. Carey's expectation of herself to do all these things triggered both feelings of powerlessness to accomplish them and relief when Fr. Bob took Ms. S. to get her dogs' shots. It seems, too, that Carey places a different value on cleanliness than does Ms. S.

The issues or values being asserted within this situation are influenced by cultural factors—economic, political, social, ethnic, gender and generational. These are often multi-layered and complex. Yet they must be addressed because of their significant influence on the people involved. How are these factors affecting the issues or values present in this situation?

Social factors which come to bear on Carey's case include Ms. S's reliance on public aid and Carey's inexperience in working with the public aid system; Ms. S.'s single status at age 63; and her interest in making "even more of a connection" at the church.

Step 5: *Create an image or metaphor based on this event.*

Up to this point you have attended to an experience by recalling its specific details and your accompanying feelings, both physical and emotional. The point to *Step 5* is to create an image of your original experience which will help "open it up" so that its meaning can be more easily drawn forth. You have also taken note of the issues or values involved. The image, or symbol, will allow you to stay in touch with the emotional intimacy of the event while creating cognitive distance. In other words, it will give your mind some space to listen to what your heart has to say.

One way to draw forth an image from your experience is by completing this statement: "Being in this situation was like. . . ." Examples of responses here: ". . . being a 'wounded healer'"; ". . . riding a roller-coaster; ". . . the story of 'The Emperor's New Clothes.' " Just let your thoughts flow, keeping in mind the dynamics of the situation.

Here are a few images drawn from Carey's story. Being in this situation was like:

A. Finding a diamond in the rough; i.e., looking beyond the appearance to the treasure within.

B. Watching the Chicago Cubs play baseball; i.e., not much to cheer about, but you've just got to love 'em!

C. Being a handcuffed lumberjack in the middle of a forest; i.e., What is my relationship to this situation when what I think I have to offer is not what is being called upon.

D. Being Martha in the story from Luke's Gospel, in which Martha does the housework while Mary sits at Jesus' feet; i.e., what is most important in being with this person?

The image or symbol you create will be related to that aspect of the story which has the most energy for you. Image A above, for example, emphasizes the surprise Carey experienced in being attracted to Ms. S. in the midst of the "chaos." Image C puts more emphasis on the fact that Carey felt powerless to do anything about this situation.

Images allow for creative responses to the operative dynamics within a situation. They "surprise and startle, please and perturb."[3] Begin by asking yourself, what is it like inside this image. For example, what is it like "finding a diamond in the rough." At first, you may be surprised that a thing of beauty is present amid the rough. You are pleased at finding something valuable.

But then, you wonder how you can get the diamond out of the rough so that you can appreciate its full beauty. What force will it take to get the diamond out? What will happen to the diamond?

By playing with the image, alternative ways of being with the other may arise. It can be interesting to look at your image again when you reach Step 8 of this process, to see if it still fits, or how you have altered it. You may come up with an entirely new image.

Images can be expressed through any of our senses—by story, drawing, music, poetry or a Scripture verse, as in Image D above—any way that helps capture the essence of this event. Keep in mind that Jesus used an imaginative tool—parables—to help his listeners approach a common occurrence in a radical way, a way which opened them to conversion. Many of his "kingdom" metaphors are good examples of this step. "The kingdom of God is like a mustard seed. . . ." "Huh? Oh . . . Yeah!"

Step 6: *Retrieve elements from our religious tradition related to this experience.*

What does this situation say about God's relationship to us? In other words, what theological point(s) does this experience bring to mind? What do I already know about that theology? What Scripture passage or religious teaching seems to be illustrated by this event?

You may come up with many theological connections, or you may only have a vague recollection of a Bible passage that seems somehow related. In the latter case, the group can help you fill in the blanks or add other ideas. For Carey, the tension between her inclination to "clean up" Ms. S's life and Fr. Bob's willingness to let Ms. S. decide what her most pressing need was, reminded her of the story of Martha and Mary in Luke's Gospel.

> Martha, who was busy with all the details of hospitality, came to Jesus and said, "Lord, are you not concerned that my sister has left me to do all the household tasks alone? Tell her to help me." The Lord in reply said to her, "Martha, Martha, you are anxious and upset about many things; one thing only is required. Mary has chosen the better portion and she shall not be deprived of it." (Lk 10:38ff)

At the heart of this "tension" is the theology of ministry, how we are called to be *with* and *for* one another. One contemporary theology of ministry recognizes the call to move beyond a philanthropic "doing for" others to a solidarity with them. For the theology of the

"Global Village," the situation of the other is understood as integrally related to our own.[4]

In responding to this step, you will draw upon your formal theological training—religion courses, Bible study, etc. It can also be helpful to have someone who is trained in theology participate in the group on some regular basis.

Step 7: *Assert the input from Step 6 with and against this event and your image of it, in order to clarify and challenge your questions, attitudes, beliefs, perceptions and ways of acting.*

Where do the story, the culture and the input from the religious tradition agree? Where do they disagree? How does my usual way of categorizing this type of event fit this time? What's different, what doesn't fit, what makes me uncomfortable?

Carey began to assert her visit with Ms. S. and the Martha and Mary story in this way:

> My first impulse is to think of all the things I should or could *do* to help this woman. But then I remember that Mary chose the better part, which is simply being with and enjoying Jesus' presence. Father Bob was very present to Ms. S; he listened to her concerns, and only followed up on *her* concerns, not necessarily his concern for her. Certainly the sense of the holy was there in his being attuned to her, and her response to him.

Carey became aware that her primary belief about ministry involved a reciprocal relationship of helper (above) doing something for client (below). In this case, however, such a notion proved inadequate in that Ms. S. was not immediately interested in what Carey was prepared to offer. Carey discovered that the boundaries of ministry are not always well defined and that people are not just interested in our helping them solve their problems.

Another question for this step is, "How would this situation have looked different in your former work place?" For example, on the psychiatric unit where Carey used to work, the relationship between staff and patient is much more rigidly defined, making her role there much less ambiguous.

Step 8: *Identify insights and questions.*

What have you become more aware of as a result of this process? What new understandings about yourself, your work, the world or the religious tradition have come to you? What have you re-learned? What questions do you still have, what new questions have arisen? What would you like to pay more attention to now?

Carey concluded her reflection with these words:

I suddenly realized I cannot contain this kind of work in any category or box. To say "yes" to relationship with the poor is to take a risk, to invite messiness, something I hate. But it also means looking at this woman in quite a different way than as a set of problems that need fixing. It is helpful to remember vocation is not a set of duties given from above, but the interplay of my gifts and weakness with another person's strengths and needs. So the question for me then becomes, "What would I most love to do with this person?"

Step 9: *Make a decision about what action to take and DO IT!*

What possible action does this reflection suggest? Make a commitment to yourself, or to the group, even if it is simply to continue reflecting.

Putting your learnings into practice is an important part of theological reflection. Attending to the events and activities that make up your ministry gives rise to new events and activities, which will hopefully be guided by the insights gained from this exercise. Carey decided to meet with Ms. S. again. She will carry with her a more probing question and a deeper awareness of the ministry of parish nursing.

A Theological Reflection Method for Health Ministry	
Step 1	Choose an event to reflect upon.
Step 2	Recall the specifics of the event.
Step 3	Recall your feelings during this event and any bodily sensations generated by it.
Step 4	Name the main issue(s) or value(s) at play in this situation, and the cultural factors affecting them.
Step 5	Create an image or metaphor based on this event.
Step 6	Retrieve elements from our religious tradition related to this experience.
Step 7	Assert the input from Step 6 with and against this event and your image of it, in order to clarify and challenge your questions, attitudes, beliefs, perceptions and ways of acting.
Step 8	Identifying insights and questions.
Step 9	Make a decision about what action to take and DO IT!

Notes

1. Robert Kinast, *Let the Ministry Teach* (Center for Theological Reflection, Madeira Beach, Florida, 1991), p. 4.

2. The Verbatim Case Study is described in "Perspectives in Parish Nursing Practice," a publication of the National Parish Nurse Resource Center.

3. Patricia O'Connell Killen uses this imagery in her courses for the Center for Development in Ministry, University of St. Mary of the Lake, Mundelein, Illinois.

4. For more on this approach, see Rebecca S. Chopp and Duane F. Parker, *Liberation Theology and Pastoral Theology*, Journal of Pastoral Care Publications, Inc., Decatur, Georgia, 1990.

Mujerista Theology's Methods: A Liberative Praxis, A Way of Life

Ada María Isasi-Díaz

MUJERISTA THEOLOGY IS A LIBERATIVE PRAXIS—REFLECTIVE ACTION THAT has as its goal the liberation of Hispanic women. *Mujerista* theology reflects upon and articulates the religious understandings and practices of Hispanic Women. *Mujerista* theology is a communal theological praxis that endeavors to enable Hispanic Women to be agents of our own history, to enhance our moral agency, and to design and participate in actions that are effective in our daily struggle for survival. *Mujerista* theology is a way of life, a living out of a divine call to participate in the unfolding of the kingdom of God in a very specific way.

Claiming the lived-experience of Hispanic Women as the source of *mujerista* theology calls for a theological method that not only explicitly identifies such experience, but also presents it as unmediatedly as possible. Coupled with this methodological requirement is the commitment of *mujerista* theology to provide a platform for the voices of Hispanic Women. Such requirement and commitment have led to the use of qualitative research methods to gather information, and to present it and explore it with integrity.

In this paper I discuss two qualitative research methods that I have used to gather the voices and lived-experience of Hispanic Women. I argue that *mujerista* theologians must present in our writings particular voices from the communities in which our theology is rooted. Otherwise we will run the risk either of objectifying grassroot Hispanic Women by talking about "them" and for "them," or we will speak exclusively for and by ourselves instead of providing a forum for the theological voice of our communities. Only if *mujerista* theology is a theological discourse that serves as a platform for oppressed Hispanic Women's voices can it claim to be a liberative praxis.

Sociological Methods and Theories

Precisely because of the absence of Hispanic Women's voices from theological discourses, our lives, our understandings, and meanings are what *mujerista* theology seeks to bring to light. But as important as bringing them to light is the way in which this is done. Often we have seen the experiences of other marginalized groups, including Hispanics, molded to fit into the accepted formats of theological discourse. We believe this has led to distortions that have resulted in new ways of silencing these groups, such as using their experiences as examples to illumine answers to questions determined by those who control the systems, while never allowing the marginalized groups to pose the questions. To avoid this, when considering what method to use in elaborating *mujerista* theology, we have kept in mind two things. First, the moral agency of Hispanic Women has to be the determining factor in our methodological considerations. Therefore, second, though we understand the elaboration itself of *mujerista* theology to be a liberative praxis, *mujerista* theology as a discourse cannot be considered more important than Hispanic Women's development as agents of our own lives and of our own history.

In struggling to maintain Hispanic Women as agents and subjects, instead of making them into objects, *mujerista* theologians discovered that we needed the voices of Hispanic Women themselves to be present in the theological discourse. These voices do not claim to be representative. Neither are they to be understood as examples of a worldview or perspective. We believe that the voices of particular Hispanic Women have validity in themselves and that without claiming to be representative they point to the reality of all Hispanic Women because they make our reality more understandable. Instead of attempting to present a universal voice, our attempt has been to point to the universal by being as specific as possible. Just as radical immanence is a different way of understanding what up to now has been called transcendence, so, too, the more specific and particular the voices we present in *mujerista* theology, the more they encompass the reality of all Hispanic Women.

But we realized this was not enough when we saw that no matter how faithfully we present specific Hispanic Women's voices, there are always numerous mediations that tend to muffle them. We also had, first of all, to investigate and understand—an ongoing process that we do not think will ever end—who we are, how we understand ourselves and elaborate meaning for ourselves. Understanding our Hispanic-ness, our ethnicity, as a social construct and identifying the key elements in it has helped us to grasp better our world and the situation of oppression in which Hispanic Women live. The second element has to do with the dialogic relationship those of us conducting the research and doing the writing of *mujerista* theology have established with the Hispanic Women whose voices we include in our discourse. Furthermore, a very important role here also is the role our religious understandings and practices play in *mujerista* theology.

Third, we have worked with the women whose voices we include so that the process of gathering the voices helps them to understand better their daily struggle to survive. Our attempt has been not to turn them into "types" but to see them as they see themselves, as persons who seek to know the meaning of their lives out of their daily struggles.[1] One of our goals has been to enable the development of their moral agency not by analyzing their religious understandings and practices but rather by seeing how they construct those understandings and practices.

Our methods have had as their objective to help these women come to know themselves, to know what they think about questions of ultimate meaning, and how these questions are used in Hispanic Women's everyday struggle to survive in the midst of great oppression. One of our objectives has been to hold up our everyday religious practices and to value them. Grounding our methods has been the firm conviction that our task is not to present already fixed representations, "pretheorized reality."[2] On the contrary, our insistence on presenting the voices of Hispanic Women has been to destabilize the balance of power and knowledge that exists between Hispanics and the dominant groups in the U.S.A., and between Hispanic Women and women of the dominant groups in the U.S.A. Such destabilizing will make possible—at the same time that it is partially caused by—the critical consciousness and practice of Hispanic Women.[3]

Gathering and presenting their voices allows Hispanic Women to be subjects of their own history, to see and present themselves as moral agents with a critical consciousness. It also makes it possible for them to understand and to present to others "powerful and insightful commentaries on the social order" that are embedded in their self-disclosing discourse. What they have shared in their narratives they understand as relating not just to themselves. They understand who they are and what they go through as something that goes beyond them, as something that has to do with the Hispanic community at large and with the whole of society.

As we gather and present the voices of grassroot Hispanic Women, *mujerista* theologians have come to understand more clearly that the conceptual frameworks and epistemological presuppositions of the world of theology cannot hold the meaning of our daily lives and our concerns, knowledge, and understandings of the divine without distorting them. The old wineskins cannot hold new wine, but if by chance they do, the new wine will turn into vinegar!

Ethnography

Mujerista theology recognizes and makes explicit the culture of the community out of which it arises, the Hispanic culture. It is appropriate, therefore, for those of us doing *mujerista* theology to avail ourselves of the techniques and principles of qualitative research which is concerned with coming to know by "watching people in their own territory and interacting with them in their own language, on their own terms."[4] The test of whether or not what one has observed corresponds to the self-understanding of the person being described is critical. In the case of the written accounts of *mujerista* theology, the test will be whether or not Hispanic Women can say, "Yes, this is my life, this is what I understand, this is what I mean."[5]

Of the different methods used in qualitative research, ethnography is one particularly well suited to doing *mujerista* theology. It is used by social sciences to describe and classify cultures by dealing with the distinctive characteristics and customs of those cultures. Ethnography is a way of conducting research that has as its foundation "the complex relationship between the researcher and his [sic] informants."[6] Ethnographical principles call for participation of the informants, of those who are being studied, in developing the method used. Ethnography calls for as little mediation as possible in describing and making known the culture in question.

Using ethnographic principles, *mujerista* theology presents the understandings and opinions of Hispanic Women, as much as possible, in their own words. To do this we conduct ethnographic interviews. These interviews are much more a conversation, a dialogue, than the standard survey form of questions and answers. In contrast to other kinds of interviews, ethnographical interviews have as their goal "to learn from people, to be taught by them,"[7] instead of just gathering information about them. This learning from the people occurs in the dialogic process that takes place between the researcher and the informants. Ethnographic interviews also make it possible to hear many voices instead of only the voices of the leaders of the community. They provide an opportunity for different members of the community to reflect on their experiences, to grasp better what they believe and how those beliefs impact their everyday lives. The interviews, therefore, are part of a liberative praxis; they are a consciousness raising experience for Hispanic Women not only because it gives them an opportunity for reflection but also because they are often a vehicle for Hispanic Women to develop their own voices. Without this voice-of-one's-own, Hispanic Women are not able to be agents of our own history.[8]

In doing *mujerista* theology I have conducted ethnographic interviews in two different settings. One is what the women who participated called "retreats," that is, reflection done in community during a weekend. The information gathered during these weekends has proved to be extremely rich. The women sparked and challenged each other to become more and more reflective and explicit about their experiences and understandings. These weekends have included celebrations as well as the development of strategies for dealing with problematic circumstances at home, in the workplace, or in the community at large.[9] I prefer this way of conducting ethnographic studies.

When this process has not been possible because of lack of money or time, the interviews have been conducted individually in the homes of the Hispanic Women or wherever they have chosen. In these one-on-one interviews, as in group interviews, I have freely mixed techniques used for focused interviews, free story interviews, case studies, and life histories. Because I have an ongoing relationship with most of the Hispanic Women whose voices are heard in the studies I have done, they themselves have provided me with extensive information about their life histories and their process of socialization. The fact that I have worked with them, that we have engaged in praxis together, has helped me to comprehend better their religious understandings, and to see how those understandings motivate them and are rooted in their actions. Given the great variety among Hispanic Women, I had to make sure that the group of Hispanic Women chosen for this study were generally representative of the total population.[10]

Meta-Ethnography

Mujerista theology is shaped by the experience of a great variety of Hispanic Women with historical roots in different countries and in different socio-economic contexts. In order to bring together multiple ethnographic accounts, I use the basic understandings and techniques of meta-ethnography.[11] The meta-ethnography I use does not attempt to aggregate the information gathered in interviews but rather to interpret it. First I present the different accounts as they were actually voiced by Hispanic Women. I then attempt to bring together the single accounts by pointing out some of their commonalities and differences. This results in what meta-ethnography calls "knowledge synthesis," a synthesis which is both inductive and interpretative.[12]

This approach does not judge the religious understandings and practices of Hispanic Women, nor does it try to make them fit into traditional theological frameworks or those articulated by others. *Mujerista* theology, then, is not only concerned with theological answers but, more importantly, asks theological questions from the perspective of Hispanic Women. This approach is holistic because it takes into consideration the cultural context of Hispanic Women. In other words, it does not present their religious understandings as something apart from their day-to-day living. In fact, in many ways, *mujerista* theology is an accomplishment of everyday life.

Finally, *mujerista* theology takes into consideration alternative interpretations of the understandings and experiences of Hispanic Women. There is no desire on the part of *mujerista* theology to present a single voice. On the contrary, we recognize that differences are part of the specific identity of each person. We consider differences to be a reality which enriches our theology, helping to keep it vital and viable.

Why We Use Ethnography and Meta-Ethnography in *Mujerista* Theology

Ethnography and meta-ethnography provide understandings and techniques that make it possible to discover, organize, present, and interpret the source of *mujerista* theology: the lived-experience of Hispanic Women. The reasons for using ethnography and meta-ethnography, then, are to be found in the reasons we have for placing this lived-experience at the center of our theological task.

Though the expression "lived-experience" might seem tautological to some, in the context of *mujerista* theology it refers not only to what has happened—what a person has endured or made happen—but to that experience upon which she reflects in order to understand its significance and to value it accordingly.[13] Because of the centrality of religion in the day-to-day life of Hispanic Women, our understandings about the divine and about questions of ultimate meaning play a very important role in the process of giving significance to and valuing our experience. It is imperative for us, therefore, to comprehend better how religious understandings and practices impact our lives. In order to do this, we need to start from what we know—ourselves, our everyday surroundings and experiences.

In society the dominant understandings and practices that are considered as having important religious significance, the ones that carry weight and impact societal norms, arise from the experience of the dominant culture, class, race, and gender. Whether or not those people actually invest themselves in these understandings and practices, they abide by the understandings, consciously or unconsciously. These are elements of the structures that keep them in power. By using our lived-experience as the source of theology, Hispanic Women start from a place outside those structures, outside the traditional theology which is controlled by the dominant group. This gives us an opportunity to be self-defining, to give fresh answers, and, what is most important, to ask new questions.

For us who do *mujerista* theology it is essential to look at the questions being asked in theology.[14] Our task, in general, is not that of answering centuries-old questions from a different perspective without looking at the questions themselves. Our task is not to use grassroot Hispanic Women's answers to old questions. This results in so-called "new" answers, which are most often nothing but reinterpretations of old answers, old answers with different words and different emphases, but basically within the parameters of the old answers. We consciously seek to avoid manipulating what grassroot Hispanic Women say to fit the parameters established by traditional questions and "old" answers.

For example, some Hispanic theologians give great importance to Scripture. Their goal is to present Jesus in such a way that the common folk can relate to him. Undoubtedly, the experience of Hispanics also plays a part in the hermeneutical work of these theologians. But in their work, the fact that the great majority of Hispanics relate very little to Jesus is never confronted. Instead, it is glossed over. This results, therefore, in a "new" emphasis on Jesus but never in new questions about Jesus or about how Jesus has been used by theologians and those with power in the churches to oppress and marginalize Hispanic Women.[15]

Mujerista theology, on the other hand, using the lived-experience of Hispanic Women as its main source, pushes out the old parameters and insists on new questions. In the case of Jesus, for example, we ask Why is it that the majority of Hispanic Women do not relate to Jesus? What does this mean about their understanding of the divine and the presence of the divine in their lives? *Mujerista* theology, then, often becomes a subversive act by enabling Hispanic Women to be suspicious of what we have not participated in defining.

A third reason for insisting on the lived-experience of Hispanic Women as a source for *mujerista* theology concerns our struggle for liberation and our sanity. As people who live submerged within a culture which is not ours, we often question our ability to comprehend "reality." In a very real way, as Hispanic Women, we have to "go out of our minds" in order to survive physically.[16] You can often hear Hispanic Women, especially older women, respond to "that's the way things are done here," with the phrase, *en qué cabeza cabe eso?*, in what kind of head does that fit? The reality that impacts our daily lives is often incomprehensible to us. What we say does not count; our cultural customs—dance, food, dress—are divorced from us and are commercialized; our values hardly count in society; our language is considered a threat, and millions have voted to have Spanish declared "not an official language"; our social reality is ignored. As a people we continue to slip into poverty and to suffer from the social ills prevalent in the culture of poverty.

By using our lived-experience as the source of *mujerista* theology, we are trying to validate our world, our reality, our values. We are trying to reverse the schizophrenia that attacks our lives by insisting that who we are and what we do is revelatory of the divine. The lived-experience of Hispanic Women constitutes our common and shared reality. The "common sense" of Hispanic Women is not wrong. We can trust it to inform and guide our day-to-day life. *Mujerista* theology wants to affirm the worldview of Hispanic Women, shaped as it is by our lived-experience. For it is precisely in our worldview, in our paradigm of social reality, that we find "the categories and concepts through and by which we construct and understand the world,"[17] and understanding and constructing our world is a liberative praxis.

Finally, what much of the above implies is that the centrality of the lived-experience of Hispanic Women in *mujerista* theology is based on what liberation theologies call the epistemological privilege of the poor and the oppressed. This privilege is not based on the moral or intellectual superiority of the oppressed; it does not mean that Hispanic Women personally are better or more innocent or more intelligent or purer in our motivations. No, this epistemological privilege is based on the possibility the oppressed have

> to see and to understand what the rich and the powerful cannot see nor understand. It is not that their sight is perfect, it is the place where they are which makes the difference. Power and richness have a distortionary effect—they freeze our view of reality. The point of view of the poor, on the other hand, pierced by suffering and attracted by hope, allows them, in their struggles, to conceive another reality. Because the poor suffer the weight of alienation, they can conceive a different project of hope and provide dynamism to a new way of organizing human life *for all.*[18]

The lived-experience of Hispanic women, therefore, brings a new dynamism to theology. It is our lived-experience which allows us to conceive another theological reality, a new theological reality, a liberative praxis, which we call *mujerista* theology.

Reprinted by permission from *En La Lucha* by Ada María Isasi-Díaz, copyright© 1993 Augsburg Fortress.

Notes

1. Ruth Behar, "Rage and Redemption: Reading the Life Story of a Mexican Marketing Woman," *Feminist Studies* 16, no. 2 (summer 1990), p. 230.

2. Ibid., p. 230.

3. Ibid., p. 231.

4. Jerome Kirk and Marc L. Miller, *Reliability and Validity in Qualitative Research*, Qualitative Research Methods 1 (Beverly Hills, CA: Sage Publications, 1986), p. 9.

5. See Harold Garfinkel, *Studies in Ethnomethodology* (Cambridge, England: Polity Press, 1984), pp. 1-115. See also, Thomas Dale Watts, "Ethnomethodology: A Consideration of Theory and Research," *Cornell Journal of Social Relations* 9, 1 (Spring 1973), pp. 99-115.

6. James P. Spradley, *You Owe Yourself a Drunk—An Ethnography of Urban Nomads* (Boston: Little, Brown and Company, 1970), p. 7.

7. James P. Spradley, *The Ethnographic Interview* (New York: Holt, Rinehart and Winston, 1979), p. 4.

8. Ethnographic interviews are only one of the tools used by *mujerista* theology. Observation, studies of traditional religious understandings and beliefs, studies in comparative religions—all of these are also tools used by *mujerista* theology.

9. I am referring here to the research done for this book and the one we did for the book Ada María Isasi-Díaz and Yolanda Tarango, *Hispanic Women: Prophetic Voice in the Church* (Minneapolis, MN: Fortress, 1992).

10. I never ask the Latinas I interview if they are Roman Catholic. However, that is my own faith tradition and the church in which I have worked in different ways for many years. Also, most of the women I have worked with in articulating a *mujerista* theology are Roman Catholic. On the other hand, most of my work in the decade of the 1980s was in ecumenical settings. This allowed me to come in contact with and learn from Hispanic Women who belong to Protestant denominations and also to Pentecostal churches.

11. Though basically following the understandings and techniques explained in the works quoted in this section, I have also adapted meta-ethnography according to values I hold as a *mujerista* theologian.

12. George W. Noblit and R. Dwight Hare, *Meta-Ethnography: Sythesizing Qualitative Studies*, Qualitative Research Methods, Vol. II (Beverly Hills, CA: Sage Publications, 1988), p. 16.

13. Following Gramsci, I believe that action has a reflective quality. This assertion is very important for Hispanics because U.S.A. society tends to disregard our intellectual ability due to a certain lack of formal education. Following Gramsci I claim that Hispanic Women are organic thinkers and that *mujerista* theology, which is based on "the principles and problems raised . . . by their practical activity," is organic theology. See Antonio Gramsci, *Prison Notebook*, ed. and trans. Quintin Hoare and Geoffrey Nowell Smith (New York: International Publishers, 1975), pp. 6, 330.

14. As Rosaldo said, "What is needed . . . is not so much data as questions." M. Z. Rosaldo, "The Use and Abuse of Anthropology: Reflections on Feminism and Cross-Cultural Understanding," *Signs* 5 (Spring 1980), p. 390.

15. See Virgilio Elizondo, *Galilean Journey: The Mexican-American Promise* (Maryknoll, NY: Orbis Books, 1983).

16. The first person I ever heard give this expression the interpretation I present here was Barbara Zanotti, who together with me and four other women participated in a dialogue with United States Bishops on the issue of the ordination of women in the Roman Catholic Church at the beginning of the 1980s.

17. Liz Stanley and Sue Wise, *Breaking Out: Feminist Consciousness and Feminist Research* (London: Routledge & Kegan Paul, 1983), p. 154. Also, Janet Silman "In Search of a Liberative Methodology," unpublished paper, May 7, 1988.

18. José Míguez Bonino, "Nuevas Tendencias en Teología," in *Pasos* 9 (1987), p. 22.

· 11 ·

Reconciliation and the Church in China

Robert Schreiter

THROUGH THE MANY CHANGES THAT HAVE TAKEN PLACE IN AND AMONG nations during the last few years, the situations in some places have dramatically improved while, in other places, they have considerably worsened. The new circumstances which such changes create often require people to come to terms with a past marred by violence, oppression and persecution. This has resulted in a call for the renewal of the ancient Christian practice of reconciliation.

In China, too, Catholics are being asked to reconcile themselves to one another and to overcome the harmful divisions that have rent the fabric of the church there for over thirty years. While the situation among China's Catholics has evolved since 1958, there are still many hurdles to cross. Two questions arise: Is reconciliation possible; and if so, how will it happen?

On the one hand the word "reconciliation" is often used in two different ways. Sometimes it is used easily and quickly—too easily perhaps. People using it in this fashion think that reconciliation is something that can be effected quickly, if only the offending party would apologize, and the offended party would extend forgiveness. Rarely, if ever, are long and painful histories so easily resolved.

On the other hand, the word "reconciliation" is sometimes introduced into a situation with great care, since the users of that word know what will be entailed. The task can be so daunting that all parties feel paralyzed.

It is probably better to err on the side of caution in these matters. Yet we need not be paralyzed in the situation. There are things
that we can do, attitudes that we can cultivate, steps that we can
take. In this article, I would like to explore the biblical understanding of reconciliation as a basis for looking forward to a time of
reconciliation for the Catholic church in China.

Needless to say, the situation of the church in China is very
complex; it varies from place to place; and is always changing. Nor
is it a simple matter of good versus evil, for there are people of good
will on both sides, people who have borne the burden of history as
best they know how. Yet many divisions remain—perhaps not as
sharp as they once were, but problematic and unresolved nonetheless. And there remain long, painful histories that must be faced and
somehow reconciled.

Reconciliation is one of those themes in the Scriptures that is
clearly very central to understanding what God has done for the
world in Christ, and yet surprisingly little is actually said directly
about it. Most of what we do have, is found in the Pauline and Deuteropauline materials. Here we are reminded that the reconciliation
of a sinful world unto God is the very reason for Christ's having
come among us. We are told, further, that reconciliation has already
taken place through the blood of his cross, although the complete
achievement of that reconciliation still lies before us. What its full
realization will look like is given to us only in glimpses; however, it
will take shape and it will involve all things, "whether above the
earth, on the earth or under the earth."

I would like to explore this message of Christian reconciliation,
since it is the source of a profound hope that can sustain Christians
who now suffer from the struggle with their divisions. I wish to do
this by looking at three dimensions of the message: first, what reconciliation is not, lest we confuse it with other dynamics in our
world and put our hopes in the wrong place; secondly, what can be
distilled from the Scriptures, especially from the Pauline corpus, of
the meaning of Christian reconciliation; and finally, what this may
suggest for our consideration of reconciliation for the church in
China.

What Reconciliation Is Not

There is some advantage in beginning our reflections on Christian reconciliation by stating what it is not, since the word itself can
mean so many different things. We speak, after all, of reconciling
bank statements, labor disputes, divorce suits, and arguments.

There are three ways in which the term reconciliation is commonly understood that do not reflect, as such, its Christian or biblical understanding. These three are: reconciliation as a hasty peace, reconciliation as an alternative to liberation, and reconciliation as a managed process.

Reconciliation as a hasty peace tries to deal with a history of pain and suffering by suppressing its memory and ignoring its effects. It tries to put behind us that painful and difficult story and urges a fresh beginning on all sides. Not surprisingly, this version of reconciliation is invoked often by the very ones who have perpetrated the suffering or by those who have quietly stood by as it happened. They want the victims of that history to let bygones be bygones and exercise a "Christian forgiveness."

By trivializing the suffering of others in this way, these false attempts at reconciliation actually underscore how far the situation still is from genuine reconciliation. But calling on those who have suffered to forget or overlook their suffering, is in fact to continue the oppressive situation by saying, in effect, that the experiences of those who have suffered are not important—indeed, that they themselves are unimportant to the reconciling process. By forgetting the suffering with such haste, the victim is forgotten and the causes of suffering are never uncovered or confronted.

Unfortunately, church people can easily find themselves implicated in this kind of false reconciliation. They naturally feel constrained to speak a word of peace and bring to bear the resources of the Christian message on a troubled situation. But if those same church people have not been part of the struggle, have contented themselves with standing outside or above the situation while making pronouncements about it, they end up, albeit unintentionally, part of the problem rather than part of its solution. This was the accusation leveled by the authors of the *Kairos* Document at church leaders with their "church theology" in South Africa in 1985.[1] One cannot come into the final act of a drama and expect to play a leading role.

Secondly, reconciliation is not an alternative to liberation. In 1985, a concerted effort was made by some conservative bishops and theologians in Latin America to replace theologies of liberation with a theology of reconciliation, claiming that this would be more faithful to the spirit of the gospel. The Los Andes Declaration emanating from a conference held in Chile that year made a case for this kind of thinking.[2]

To the minds of its authors reconciliation captured more fully the finality of the Christian message, and was not as conflictual as liberation. It offered peace to all sides.

This form of reconciliation, like reconciliation as a hasty peace, does echo something of the Christian message. But it too obscures the very causes of conflict and suffering and therefore does not bring about a true reconciliation. Put simply, liberation is not an alternative to reconciliation, it is its prerequisite. Not: liberation *or* reconciliation. Rather: *no* reconciliation *without* liberation. Reconciliation instead of liberation fails to recognize the dimensions of the conflict, especially when the causes of the conflict are hidden and the violence perpetrated is covert in nature. It also ignores the fact that division is not peripheral or an epiphenomenon arising out of a conflictual situation, but is something that stands at the very heart of it. To ignore the division is to ignore the situation, and no alternative remedies can begin to undo the situation.

Finally, reconciliation is not a managed process, like arbitration. Reconciliation is not conflict-mediation, a process whose goal is to lessen conflict or to get the conflicted parties to live with the conflictual situation. Conflict-mediation tries to get both parties to surrender some claims in the hope of reducing tensions, but not so many that tensions are heightened instead. Such conflict-mediation may be and often is necessary in this fallen world, but it should not be confused with reconciliation just because it brings about a temporary cessation in hostilities. As we shall see, for the Christian, reconciliation is not a skill to be mastered; but rather something to be discovered: the power of God's grace welling up in one's life. Reconciliation becomes more of an attitude than an acquired skill; it becomes a stance assumed before a broken world rather than a tool to repair that world. Or put in theological terms, reconciliation is more of a spirituality than a strategy.

These three ways of misunderstanding reconciliation—as a hasty process, as an alternative to liberation, and as a managed process—should alert us to how complex the reality of reconciliation actually is. In a way, we, as Christians, should not be surprised. For reconciliation stands at the heart of the Good News we preach: God's plan for creation and Christ's central work within that plan. Let us turn now to a distillation of that biblical message.

The Christian Message of Reconciliation

Although the concept of reconciliation is central to Christian understanding of what God has done for the world in Christ, the term "reconciliation" itself does not occur that frequently in the Bible. It does not occur at all in the Hebrew Scriptures, although it is no doubt implied in the concept of atonement. Paul is the principal source of its usage in the New Testament, and even there it occurs in some form only fourteen times. The verb "to reconcile," *katallassein*, was understood in Paul's time in a secular context, meaning a making of peace after a time of war.

This is not the place to engage in a prolonged exegesis of the passages related to this concept in the authentic Pauline and the Deuteropauline letters. That has been done competently and comprehensively elsewhere.[3]

Let me rather try to distill from these texts five essential elements which give us a picture of how reconciliation is to be understood from a Christian perspective.

First of all, *it is God who initiates and brings about reconciliation.* We humans are not in a position, either as victims or oppressors, to recreate ourselves in such a way as to overcome completely the damage done by situations of conflict and violence. While we may surmount these situations, we seem never to be liberated completely. We are never quite able to get things completely right, perhaps because the effects of conflict and division have seeped too deeply into our bones. This is not said to encourage fatalism or quietism, for we are indeed invited by God to cooperate in God's reconciling ways. It is simply to remind us from whence reconciliation comes and who continues to guide it.

Secondly, *reconciliation is more a spirituality than a strategy.* Reconciliation is not brought about by a technical, problem-solving rationality as much as by embracing a view of the world that recognizes and responds to God's reconciling action. Reconciliation is discovered in the justifying and reconciling grace of God welling up in our lives and in our communities. It is from the experience that we are able to go forth in a ministry of reconciliation. Reconciliation becomes a vocation, a way of life, and not just a set of discrete tasks to be performed and completed. Reconciled communities and individuals do not return to a pre-conflictual state, they live in a new kind of way.

Thirdly, *reconciliation makes of both victim and oppressor a new creation.* What reconciliation is about is more than righting wrongs and repenting evildoing. These are surely included, but the biblical understanding of reconciliation sees that we are indeed taken to a new place, and become a new creation. Reconciliation is not just restoration; it brings us to a place where we have not been before. This becomes important because we often harbor preconceived notions of what the reconciled state will be like. The Scriptures remind us that we will be more than restored, we will be a new creation.

Fourthly, *the story that overcomes the story of division and violence is the story of the passion, death and resurrection of Jesus.* In this story, God in Christ enters into the depths of the story of human suffering, of conflict and of division. Body, blood and cross are the symbols that recur over and over in that story, symbols that can bear the paradox of the transformation of suffering and death into a new story of deliverance and life. The violence of our situations is met with the violence of Jesus' death; the dawning of the resurrection heralds that "new place" where the reconciled are gathered. The symbol of Christ's body is the vehicle for restoring the shattered bodies of those who suffer, and for gathering the scattered community of those driven apart in violence and conflict. The symbol of blood carries the memories of violence to be healed. It portends new life to those who have shed their own blood. The symbol of the cross exposes the lie of human power and domination, and the truth of how human designs often go deeply awry. The cross challenges our understandings of what constitutes power in this world, understandings that make violence and oppression possible.

And finally, *reconciliation embraces all dimensions of reality.* Reconciliation breaks down human enmity, and embraces the entire cosmos. It acknowledges that the reconciling process reaches beyond God's reconciling offer. It points to the alienation yet to be overcome. It involves laments for what has been lost and calls forth a healing memory. It has cosmic dimensions that we only dimly understand.

This, perhaps all too succinctly, tries to bring together an understanding of God's reconciling activity in the world as presented in the Pauline corpus. It remains for us to see what this means for us as Christians and our vocation as the bearers of God's Good News.

Reconciliation and the Church in China

What meaning might all this have for the eventual reconciliation of the church in China? A number of suggestions follow that are drawn from what has been said above and are offered as possible points for reflection to those who wish to be part of the reconciliation process. They are based on a Christian understanding of reconciliation, and not on the particular experience of someone who knows the China situation well. For this reason, they are offered rather as a resource to those who are closer to the situation than is this author.

First of all, it is important to realize that the reconciliation process usually begins with the victim, not with the oppressor. We usually suppose that reconciliation begins when the oppressor repents of evildoing and seeks the victim's forgiveness. In the Christian view, however, it is the other way around. What happens is that the shattered victim discovers God's offer of healing grace and accepts God's favor as a restoration of an abused and shattered humanity. This is not the blaming-the-victim syndrome. Rather, it represents God's being on the side of the little one, the *anawim*, giving them the strength to overcome the mighty. God rescues the humanity of the victim, a humanity of which the victim has been robbed by violence. The forgiveness that the victim is now able to offer as a result of having experienced God's care and healing, is what will provoke repentance on the part of the oppressor. This is captured beautifully in the words of Joe Seramane, now Director of the Justice and Reconciliation Department of the South Africa Council of Churches. Bearing witness to justice led to his imprisonment and torture. After his release, he was able to meet with his torturer once again and to offer him this forgiveness. He tells us now that "it is through reconciliation that we regain our humanity. To work for reconciliation is to live to show others what their humanity is."

In the situation of Catholics, and indeed all Christians, in China, who is the victim and who the oppressor? Those communities that the government has officially recognized are sometimes identified with the oppressors, and those that are still outlawed and persecuted as the victims. But such quick designations may no longer be accurate. What may be more important is to ask: who have felt the reconciling grace of God within their hearts? Who, in experiencing that grace, have seen how they have been diminished by the experience of the last thirty years and yet also see how God is at work healing that history? It is those who are experiencing God's work in their hearts who will be the leaders in the reconciliation process. They will be able to echo the sentiments of Joe Seramane quoted above. No one can appoint oneself as a reconciling agent; only God can do that.

Second, there is no reconciliation without liberation. While there is tolerance of religion in China, there are limits to that toleration. Church people are not yet completely free to act as they choose. For that reason, we should not be surprised if full reconciliation will remain unlikely for as long as certain restraints remain in place. There can be no full reconciliation without truth. It likewise reminds us of how long the reconciliation process may take and, again, that reconciliation is principally the work of God.

Third, reconciliation will make of the church in China a new creation. It will not be a matter of reverting to a former pre-1958 style, nor of one side assuming the form and style of the other. God's reconciling work makes of us a new creation. I would suggest that one place to look for the newness of creation will be in how the word "Catholic" is understood. The root of the word is "holos," meaning a sense of the whole. What will the "whole" be for Catholics in this new creation? In a sense the very name "Catholic" implies a search for and a responsibility to the whole. Might not such a quest—to search and care for the whole in order to be truly Catholic—be our motivation in the reconciliation process?

Fourth, the divisions are only likely to be overcome if they are somehow brought into contact with the three great reconciling symbols of the New Testament: the body of Christ, crucified and glorified; the blood of Christ, poured out in suffering and now the drink of the everlasting kingdom; and the cross, that exposes the lies of the world and which has become the throne of God. Divisions have within themselves deep paradoxes. The paradoxical nature of the great reconciling symbols of body, blood and cross may be what is needed to overcome the suffering of the past and the divisions the past has engendered.

Fifth, and finally, reconciliation is not merely a moment in the healing of a divided church. It is as close as we can come to God's very action within and among us. God's work in Christ is described as God's reconciling the world to God's self. We are called to be ministers of reconciliation (2 Cor. 5:20), but not on our own power: only as ambassadors on Christ's behalf. In experiencing reconciliation, we experience the most intimate movement of God in our lives. Thus for the church in China to desire reconciliation is more than a wish to overcome a sad and painful past; it is the yearning to feel the touch of God.

Reconciliation is not an easy process. But if we yearn and pray for it, we can have confidence that God will hear our prayer. We need also to look for signs of hope. John Baptist Jiang reported in *The Clergy Review* (no. 299) that in one place in China two bishops are sharing the same house: one a bishop of the "official" church recognized by the government, the other from the "unofficial" church. They are also said to share some measure of "communion" with one another.[4] Whatever that might mean precisely, it does show that there is indeed hope. But we must seek God's reconciling grace in our lives, face the truth that sets us free from suffering and painful memories, and prepare ourselves to become a new creation.

Notes

1. "The *Kairos* Document: Challenge to the Church," *Journal of Theology for Southern Africa*, no. 53 (1985), pp. 51-81.

2. "Declaración de Los Andes," *Mensaje* 34 (1985), pp. 399-402.

3. See especially Cilliers Breytenbach, *Versöhnung. Eine Studie zur paulinischen Soteriologie* (Neukirchen-Vluyn: Neukirchener Verlag, 1989); and Jose Comblin, "O Tema de reconciliação e a Teologia na América Latina, *Revista Eclesiástica Brasileira* 46 (1986), pp. 272-314, upon which the following remarks are based.

4. Cited in Aloysius B. Chang, "The Bridge Church: Christianity in China," *Catholic International* 2 (1991), p. 924; also *Tripod*, 61 (1991), pp. 6-16.

• Conclusion •

The Play of Pastoral Reflection

THE SEARCH CONTINUES FOR NEW IMAGES AND METAPHORS TO GUIDE the practice of theological reflection. We seek models that are at once lively and truthful—that better reveal us to ourselves and that energize us for our pursuit and profession.

This effort to re-imagine what we are about is aided by a renewed interest among theologians in the imagination as a creative resource.[1] Once considered either a passive abode in which sense perceptions were rearranged, or as a dangerous source of sexual temptations and aggressive fantasies, imagination is being recovered as a constructive source of religious faith. Faith is the surprising ability and gift to imagine or construe life in a certain fashion. A believer is precisely a person with a certain kind of imagination: one which envisions directions and purposes where the unbeliever sees only random activity or instinctual drives. The image, so popular today, of a "journey of faith" is just that—an image that perceives links between disparate events and finds a coherent direction among the many surges and reversals which constitute any human life. When we talk of "models and styles" of theological reflection, we are speaking about our imagination. How do we envision what we are about?

The Play of Three Authorities

In *Method in Ministry*, we have imagined the ecclesial reflection that leads to more graceful exercises of faith as the interplay of three authorities: the Christian tradition, cultural information, and personal experience. We have spoken of this interaction as a conversation that succeeds only if the three partners engage one another with

142

frankness and honesty. In this conclusion we bring our conversation to a close with a reflection on the metaphor of play.

When we engage in a corporate reflection on some significant question for Christian life, a discernment which intends to move through clarification and purification toward some practical, graceful action, what are we doing? We want to suggest that what we are doing is playing. The paradigm of play has been gaining increasing attention and favor in philosophy, psychology, and theology as we better recognize the role of imagination in interpretation and the play involved in any conversation. Theologian John Dominic Crossan suggests that play is more than a metaphor; it is, in fact, a "metaphor of metaphors,"[2] a comprehensive image of human living. We would suggest, as well, that play is an appropriate image for practical ecclesial reflection.

Images of Creation

Christians most often imagine creation as God's accomplished production. We find ourselves within a finished habitat. In such a stable environment the challenge is to understand and obey the rules (the natural law) which govern the creatures of this world. In such a picture of reality we expect to find little "play" or leeway. Such play would infer a wobbly creation, a faulty design—an insult to its crafter. In such a creation our most creative acts are re-creative, re-productive; we re-do what has been fully and perfectly modeled for us in the original creation. This vision of life imparts a sacred privilege to origins and will likely elicit nostalgia as we seek to emulate God's original plans for us. Adam and Eve's naming of the animals, a playful interpretation left to them in an unfinished creation, hints at this model's insufficiency.

Creation has also been envisioned by Christians as something to be *worked*. This industrial metaphor grows out of a specific interpretation of the original creation in a six-day (work) week. There is more room for human creativity in this model of creation since we are co-creators, taking up where God left off (after a rest day on the Sabbath). How fully accomplished creation was during that first fateful week is debatable; thus some play appears between our work and God's. But the chief characteristic of this paradigm may be its seriousness. This sober model has had great influence in the industrial West. It combines creativity with a lack of playfulness. Implications of such a purposeful paradigm are that creation (and our creative works) is not for its own sake but for something else (e.g., heaven), and that it need not involve delight or pleasure.

A third, less common image of creation envisions creation as something being *played*. The chief characteristics of this model are the incompletion of reality, waiting to be further imagined and played, and the delight and risk of such ongoing invention.

The image of creation as play is an ancient one. "All the world's a stage" is a cherished vision of reality, but one which we have most often interpreted as an invitation to play out already fully scripted roles. The delight and inventiveness of play in this traditional interpretation (even an explicit script leaves some room or play for different intonations and gestures) is that of mimesis, rather than any radical creativity. The eternal author and temporal performers are sharply and clearly distinguished.

Plato would combine the image of play with a conviction about a fully accomplished reality: "All of us, then, men and women alike, must fall in with our role and spend life making our play [*paidiàs*] as perfect as possible" (*Laws* 7, 803c). The clues to Plato's deepest conviction about reality lie, of course, in the words "fall in with" and "as perfect as possible." Human life is here understood as role-playing a part already perfectly scripted in the ideal of each vocation. This interpretation of reality is reinforced by Plato in the sentence which precedes the above: "Humans . . . have been constructed as a *plaything* of god and this is, in fact, the finest thing about them." Here creation (for the Platonic Christian) is interpreted as God's play, with humans being passive, fully fated objects in this divine delight.

But the image of creation as play has more inventive possibilities. In play we imagine reality, and our place in it, anew. We more than imitate or reproduce; we invent. In the continuing play of creation we introduce new motifs—whether these be nuclear warfare, homosexual holiness, or women priests. If these are variations on old motifs (ancient questions of a just war, sexuality, and community leadership), they are also new. It is precisely in the leeway between the old and the new, the traditional and contemporary experience, that we play our lives. And in this interpretive play we make our lives: we *identify* ourselves. As this is true for personal development, it is the case for ecclesial reflection. The correlation we find among our tradition, our culture, and our personal experience is a more-than-imitative play; in such interpretations we imagine the next stage of the Christian tradition. We write a chapter never before existing in this literary classic.

Provocative with Pitfalls

For Western thinkers, the image of play is burdened by many cultural biases. These biases appear first in our language. One such bias is that play is childish. In classical Greek the word for "play," seen in the quote from Plato, is *paidià*; the word for children is *paidiá*, different only in accent. More than linguistically, we have emphasized childhood as the proper domain of play. Whether this is the free play of the toddler or the earnest play of the school-age child practicing for life, children and play seem made for one another. But adults are expected to set aside play. Artists and athletes are, of course, exceptions: these pretenders and "adults playing a child's game" distract us and console us during the serious exercise of our adult responsibilities.

A second bias about play is inscribed in the other language that lies at the root of Western culture. The Latin word for "play," *ludere*, has given us such words as "ludicrous" and "illusory." Such words argue the frivolous and insubstantial nature of human play. Our language trains us daily to understand play as inconsequential. "He didn't mean it; he was just playing around." When we speak about playing a role we most often mean stepping out of reality in order to impersonate, to be something unreal.

This frivolous character of play may take us in the direction of illusion and deceit; it may also lead us into sin. A famous passage in our Scriptures suggests connections between play, immorality, and even idolatry. The Israelites, unfaithful to Yahweh in Moses' absence, build a golden calf; then, "the people sat down to eat and drink, and rose up to play" (Exod. 32:6). Saint Paul quotes this passage (the only use of the verb *paízein* in the New Testament) in warning the community in Corinth to abstain from sexual immorality (1 Cor. 10:7). In both texts the "rising up to play" is a sojourn not to the tennis court or the video arcade, but to an old-fashioned debauch. Play is not only childish and unreal; it is often immoral.

Surrounded by such cultural and religious biases, can the image of play be rescued? One clue is found in Chapter 8 of the Book of Proverbs. This book, borrowing heavily from Israel's neighbors, provides a strikingly non-Israelite story of creation. Wisdom or Sophia, the feminine form of God, speaks:

I was by his side, a master crafter,
delighting him day after day,
ever at play in his presence,
at play everywhere in his world,
delighting to be with the children of humanity.
(vv. 30-31, Jerusalem Bible)

Innumerable questions, linguistic and theological, surround this text. Who is this "Sophia," companion and player with the Creator? Hebrew texts differ, some suggesting "child," others "master crafter." (See the *Jerome Biblical Commentary* 29:23; p. 500). The choice of "child" settles a number of questions: the Creator's play is with a child, not with an adult who could be construed as a consort. But apart from the non-Jewish suggestion of a female player in the creation (more appealing today than in recent millennia), the passage asserts connections among creation, play, and delight. Creation here is neither the serious production of an industrious God, nor the solitary play of a bachelor Creator. Rather it is in companionship and with delight that creation is first played.

The Leap of Theological Reflection

Play, as a paradigm both of reality and of pastoral reflection, meets its first challenge in escaping the cultural biases which beset it. It encounters its second challenge in becoming more than a rhetorical flourish, in taking on specific detail and force which rescue it from the realm of pious and pastoral jargon. Let us suggest one path to such a "toughening" of play.

Psychologist Erik Erikson takes up Plato's suggestion that play originates in the random leap of the child.[3] Erikson points to three distinct elements in such gratuitous, energetic bounds. The child leaps out of delight. Drawn by no external goal (these extrinsic ambitions—winning prizes or making money—are learned later) the child simply leaps. The leap is for its own sake, performed out of delight.

Second, the leap is a move against gravity. The child, in Erikson's phrase, "tests the leeway," challenging the gravity and givenness of life. If play is, in part, delight, it is also assertion and contest.

Third, to leap is to fall; to launch oneself upward is also to come back down to earth. Following Erikson's interpretation, we may test the adequacy of the image of play in the context of theological reflection in ministry.

We understand pastoral reflection as that process by which Christians examine some significant question of life and through clarification and purification move toward some graceful action. Such reflection happens individually, of course, in personal exercises of discernment and conscience. Here we are especially interested in its communal exercise, whether that be a reflection and action process pursued by a group of pastoral theologians, the ministry team of a parish, or a reflective community of faith. What insight can we gain by examining the corporate reflection process of Christians as a religious leap of play?

1. Play as Delight

The first element of a playful leap may be the most difficult to link to pastoral reflection. A leap is a purposeless exercise, an activity of delight undertaken for its own sake. How distant this seems from most of our efforts of communal reflection and pastoral action. Yet it may be useful to examine the leap of reflection more closely.

Genuine reflection take us beyond the status quo. We leap without knowing exactly where we will come down. To experience pastoral reflection as delightful, we must see this shared dialogue as the *stuff* of our Christian life, rather than simply a tool for achieving goals. Often we tell ourselves: if we can just resolve this debate about a just economic policy, we can get back to our usual life and duties; if we could just settle the questions of the laity's proper role, we could get on with denominational business. The image of play as an ongoing process of invigorating, exhausting leaps reminds us that such challenging exercises of reflection *are* our Christian life. Pastoral reflection is neither an emergency maneuver nor a temporary burden in Christian life; it *is* our life, what we do, who we are. In such activities we identify ourselves and imagine our religious tradition's future.

If the element of delight in play is challenging, so is the sense that play is for its own sake. As we examine the theories that underpin and undercut our practice of faith, we become more aware of the "awful purposefulness" of much Christian behavior. Our Christian heritage has a deep-running and powerful tradition about our actions being for something else: life on this earth is *for* heaven; sexual intercourse is *for* children; acts of charity are performed *for* the purpose of saving souls. Here, perhaps, our experience of liturgy can help us. Liturgy, as Romano Guardini reminds us is "pointless, but full of significance."[4] Our communal celebration of worship is ultimately for its own sake. In gratitude, reconciliation, and mourning, we celebrate the presence and power of God. We know that such celebrations effect community, but this comes as a grace of the liturgy rather than its goal.

To stress our corporate reflections as playful—exercises of delight and for their own sake—may drive us to despair. Or it may encourage us to get better at such play. If these efforts of reflection are seen not as stopgap measures to be gotten through, but as the very exercise of our faith, as how Christian life continues to be interpreted, created, and played, then we may gain more energy and wit to improve our interplay as the faith community.

2. Testing the Leeway

The second element of our playful leap is more obviously a part of theological reflection. In leaping we test the limits, exploring the "limited mobility" of our Christian lives. If the child's leap is purposeless, it does have an inner economy: to see how high, how often she can leap. Erikson finds in this aspect of the leap a model of human maturing. We always find ourselves in a context of limited mobility. Gravity restricts our leap, but not totally. The choices that craft our identity, life style, and career all occur within the limits of our personal abilities, our class and gender, and our cultural environment. It is precisely in the interplay of possibility and limit that we play out our lives. With no sense of limit we live irresponsible lives. With no sense of mobility—of possibility, of change, of newness—our lives grow stagnant, losing their flexibility and play.

Pastoral reflection happens in the interplay between the Christian tradition and contemporary experience, between theory and practice, between law and compassion. The conversation that is Christian discernment operates in this flexible interplay. The central questions facing theological reflection today contest the leeway between our religious inheritance and the demands of contemporary life. Can our conventional theories of a just war flex enough to face the drastic realities of contemporary warfare? Is there sufficient flexibility in Christian understandings of human sexuality to respond to the hopes of homosexual Christians? What leeway is there in the historical Catholic vision of priesthood that allows for an inclusion of women in this form of official ministry? In each instance we are testing the limited mobility that prevails between our heritage and present-day life. When we judge there to be no leeway in the tradition ("Christianity is hopelessly out of date"), we tend to leave the church. And we may carry with us a theology of creation that denies leeway: such flexibility may be judged an insult to the Creator, an imperfection that cannot be admitted. Instead of envisioning creation as an ongoing interpretation of who we are, we may elect a fundamentalistic view of a finished creation into which contemporary experience must obediently fit.

3. Learning How to Fall

The third aspect of the leap of faith and of theological reflection is the most poignant: in leaping we must be prepared to fall. The fortunate child learns that leaping includes falling; to fall is not a disastrous, disgracing facet of play, but an integral part of the exercise. In each leap we risk falling and failure. Both the playful child and the reflective Christian community are challenged to incorporate falling into their play. How do we learn to fall gracefully?

The challenge here concerns a theology of failure. And again it might be instructive to revisit parts of our religious tradition that imperil such a theology. In a finished creation, as we have seen, there is little room for error; movement tends to appear as infidelity and sin. A strain of perfectionism in Christian spirituality has contributed mightily to a crippling of play; in such a spirituality holiness seems to imply being fully finished, without flaw or vulnerability. No leeway survives, no playground in which to leap and test and fall.

There survive, however, within our religious heritage a few hints or clues to a theology of failure. In our Easter liturgy we recall the original Fall as a *felix culpa*. What could this mean? How can a fault, a failure of such tragic proportions, be construed as felicitous? The Christian celebration of *felix culpa* asserts that the Fall had a profound benefit: it brought the Son of God into human life. The Fall was not simply a failure, for it was fruitful. It was graceful in an ironic sense, perhaps even integral to some larger design. Could falling be part of the plot?

At both the personal and ecclesial levels we experience failure as an integral part of religious maturing. By midlife we gain the perspective (at least if we are sufficiently graced) to see the importance of the failures of our own loving and working. Our life is scarred by certain fallings; but in the graceful light of retrospection these are not all incidental or shameful. Some of these wounds have contributed in strange but tangible ways to who we now are. They seem integral to our lives: without these identifying marks we would not be who we are.

Maturity seems to demand certain "falls from grace." Some of these falls have included the wounds of personal sin; others seem to be more developmental losses—such as letting go the adolescent dreams of achievement and purifying rigid expectations of God and others. Such "de-illusionments"[5] are, perhaps, falls that are necessary for our growth.

Such developmental losses occur also in an ecclesial context. The first leaps of our childlike faith often include visions of a perfect

church, of an all-satisfying religious heritage. As we grow we are
often felled by the failures, narrowness, and even sinfulness of our
own religious tradition. These developmental falls parallel our
learning that our parents are not perfect. Maturity seems to require
that our parents and our church fail us in this way, so that we may
move toward a more adult relationship. The fruit of this maturing is
a greater tolerance for error and failure, a virtue crucial for reflection
in an adult community of faith.

A growing comfort with failure makes us more graceful players. Psychologist George Vaillant, in his *Adaptation to Life*, summa-
rizes connections among play, failure, and psychological maturity:

> It is hard to separate capacity to trust from capacity to play,
> for play is dangerous until we can trust both ourselves and
> our opponents to harness rage. In play, we must trust enough
> and love enough to risk losing without despair, to bear win-
> ning without guilt, and to laugh at error without mockery.[6]

The trust that becomes the environment of mature play develops only
as we learn to tame losing and error.

The importance of failure has a special significance in pastoral
reflection because this part of the theological enterprise is committed
to practical decision making. An unfortunate "gain" for theology, as
it became an academic discipline, was that it could now avoid practical decisions—and the embarrassing errors necessarily concomitant
with such practical activities. Academic theology today can still
avoid many falls by refusing to play in the practical arena. Pastoral
reflection does not enjoy that privilege. As such it has no choice
except to learn to fall as gracefully as possible. And in its commitment to the maturing of faith communities through group reflection,
pastoral theology can help groups of believers learn to fail well. In
the contact sport of a community reflection, we must expect to fail
and, at times, be wounded. For ourselves and our communities, we
demythologize failure and falling when we re-imagine it as an integral and unavoidable part of the play of our vocations.

Theological reflection in ministry is hard work and serious
business. But it is much more than that: it is our play in God's
creation. In the corporate reflection that shapes and deepens our life
of shared faith, we not only hold onto past truths; we re-image them.
And we test the leeway between gospel and experience, between our
high ideals and a do-able life. In the midst of this invigorating play,
we fall again and again—not such a surprising fate in a religious
tradition developed under the shadow of a cross. Doing the theology of our daily lives, we play out a drama that is both ancient and

novel: the Christian vocation has been done before, but never in quite this way.

The image of pastoral reflection as play encourages us to re-imagine the seriousness and delight of what we are about. If we can overleap our inherited biases, we may employ this metaphor to clarify and enliven our communal experience of faith.

Notes

1. See, for example, David Tracy's *The Analogical Imagination: Christian Theology and the Culture of Pluralism* (New York: Crossroad, 1981), Peter Homan's *Theology After Freud: An Interpretive Inquiry* (New York: Irvington, 1970), and John Dominic Crossan's *Cliffs of Fall: Paradox and Polyvalence in the Parables of Jesus* (New York: Seabury Press, 1980). Also see our reflections in "The Religious Imagination," *Liturgy* 5, No. 1 (Summer, 1985), pp. 54-59.

2. See p. 67 of Crossan's *Cliffs of Fall*. For similar approaches to play as a central metaphor of human life, see Jacques Ehrmann's "Homo Ludens Revisited," *Yale French Studies* 41 (1968), pp. 31-57, and Jacques Derrida's "Structures, Sign and Play in the Discourse of the Human Sciences," in *Writing and Difference*, trans. Alan Bass (Chicago: University of Chicago Press, 1978), pp. 278-93.

3. See Erik Erikson's *Toys and Reasons: Stages in the Ritualization of Experience* (New York: W.W. Norton, 1977) and D. W. Winnicott's *Playing and Reality* (New York: Basic Books, 1971).

4. This quotation appears on p. 19 of Johann Huizinga's *Homo Ludens: A Study of the Play Element in Culture* (Boston: Beacon Press, 1955). First published in 1944, Huizinga's analysis of play has become the starting point for many recent reflections.

5. See Daniel Levinson's *The Seasons of a Man's Life* (New York: Alfred A. Knopf, 1978).

6. See George Vaillant's *Adaptation to Life* (Boston: Little, Brown, 1977), p. 309.

• Contributors •

Peter K. Buttitta is Pastoral Associate of Saint Gertrude Parish, Chicago. He received the Doctor of Ministry from the University of St. Mary of the Lake, under the direction of theologian Jack Shea. His book *The Still Small Voice That Beckons* and training programs based on the method of pastoral reflection that he has developed are available through Reflection Resources (2158 Berwyn Ave, Chicago 60625)

Patricia O'Connell Killen is Associate Professor and Chair of the Department of Religion at Pacific Lutheran University, Tacoma, Washington. She is primary author of *The Art of Theological Reflection* (Crossroad, 1994) and has written numerous articles on theological reflection, women in the church, and Catholicism in the United States. For over a decade she has been involved in training leaders of theological reflection groups in the United States and the Caribbean.

Ada María Isasi-Díaz is Associate Professor of Ethics and Theology at Drew University in Madison, New Jersey. Born and raised in Cuba, she has pioneered the development of *mujerista* theology, a Hispanic Women's liberation theology. Among her significant contribution on issues of social ethics, liberation theology, and Hispanic religious consciousness is her most recent book *En La Lucha / In the Struggle: Elaborating a Mujerista Theology* (Fortress, 1992).

Robert Schreiter, C.PP.S. is professor of theology at Catholic Theological Union in Chicago. He is general editor of the Faith and Cultures Series for Orbis Books and has written, among many other books, *Constructing Local Theologies* (Orbis, 1985) and *Reconciliation* (Orbis, 1992).

William G. Thompson, S.J. teaches the New Testament at the Institute of Pastoral Studies, Loyola University of Chicago. He is the author of *The Gospels for Your Whole Life: Mark and John in Prayer and Study, Paul and His Message for Life's Journey*, and *Matthew's Story: Good News for Uncertain Times*.

Eugene C. Ulrich, Professor of Hebrew Scriptures at the University of Notre Dame, is the Chief Editor of the Biblical Dead Sea Scrolls. He is the author of *The Qumran Text of Samuel and Josephus*, numerous articles, and two volumes of *Discoveries in the Judaean Desert*, the critical edition of the Scrolls.

Evelyn Eaton Whitehead is a developmental psychologist whose professional work focuses on issues of adult maturity, the dynamics of leadership, and the social analysis of community.

James D. Whitehead is a pastoral theologian and historian of religion. His theological interests concern questions of contemporary spirituality, religious leadership, and theological reflection in ministry.

The Whiteheads are consultants in education and ministry through *Whitehead Associates*, located in South Bend, Indiana. Long associated with the Institute of Pastoral Studies at Loyola University in Chicago, they contribute regularly to ministry education and adult faith formation programs in the United States and abroad.

• Index •